Praise for
*The Fast-Track Course on
How to Write a Nonfiction Book Proposal*

"...essential, succinct guideline. This is a must-have reference book for writers...sets the industry standard."
—Bob Spear, *Heartland Reviews*

"Every writer needs a book like this. Mettee's sound, practical advice is just the ticket to make an editor welcome a writer's work! Keep the book close by, because you'll use it—guaranteed!"
—William Noble, author of *Writing Dramatic Nonfiction*

"If you follow Steve Mettee's advice in this book, you're soon going to need a copy of my book."
—John Kremer, author of *1001 Ways to Market Your Book*

"...invaluable to nonfiction writers."
—Marcia Preston, publisher, *Byline Magazine*

"Mettee cuts straight to the chase and provides a no-nonsense guide which will become a reference classic."
—Magdalena Ball, editor, *The Compulsive Reader*

"...everything you need to know to wow publishers with professionally presented proposals."
—Marc McCutcheon, author of *Damn! Why Didn't I Write That?*

"If you've got a book idea that you want to turn into a book proposal, don't waste time tunneling through a pile of writing books to find out how to do it right the first time. Instead, get Mettee's book—he's done the tunneling for you and turned the results into solid gold advice..."
—Betty Winslow, *Absolute Write*

"...I will now recommend [Mettee's] book to prospective authors .... As you would want in any book on writing, it is highly readable, well-organized and to the point."
—Marcia Yudkin, author of *Freelance Writing*

THE FAST-TRACK COURSE ON

How to Write a Nonfiction Book Proposal

Second Edition

by Stephen Blake Mettee

Fresno, California

The Fast-Track Course on How to Write a Nonfiction Book Proposal
Second Edition

Published by Quill Driver Books
An imprint of Linden Publishing
2006 S. Mary, Fresno, California 93721
559-233-6633 / 800-345-4447
QuillDriverBooks.com

Quill Driver Books and colophon are trademarks of
Linden Publishing, Inc.

ISBN 978-1-61035-050-1

First printing.

Printed in the United States of America on acid-free paper

For Josh, golf partner, business advisor, best friend, son.

Library of Congress Cataloging-in-Publication Data

Mettee, Stephen Blake, 1947-

The fast-track course on how to write a nonfiction book proposal /
Stephen Blake Mettee. -- Second edition.

pages cm. -- (Great books for writers)

Includes bibliographical references and index.

ISBN 978-1-61035-050-1 (pbk.)

1. Authorship--Marketing. 2. Book proposals. I. Title. II. Title: How
to write a nonfiction book proposal.

PN161.M485 2012

808.02--dc23

2012001619

Contents

Preface

I love going to writer's conferences. For some reason, at writer's conferences, I am far more popular than I am in real life. Writers stop me in the hall just to talk, they laugh long and hard at my jokes, and even seem to find my witty repartee, well, wittier. (I choose to ignore the possibility this is because I am a publisher to whom they may some day want to sell a book.)

I find this attention to be wonderful, because my heroes are writers—I'd rather meet the uncelebrated author of the book from which a movie is made than I would the famous actor or actress starring in the movie (with the possible exception of J Lo).

Stop and think for a minute what our modern world would be like without writers: no books, no magazines, no movies, very little news reporting—no blogs! We owe writers. So, with this debt in mind—and disregarding the fact that I enjoyed writing it and was driven by visions of great monetary reward—this book is an attempt to give something back to the writing community.

Why, you ask, write another book on writing nonfiction book proposals since, prior to the publication of this work, there were at least two excellent guides to writing book proposals on the market? Because I found each of these left out small, yet important, bits of information and included extraneous information, interesting and perhaps useful, yet only peripherally applicable to the task of writing and submitting a book proposal. And they were long. When I held one of these books up at writer's workshops, I could see eyes glaze over. "You mean I have to read a 230-page book to learn how to write a 20-page book proposal?" the participants seemed to be saying.

In fact, I found many would decide to forego reading one of these books and, thus, would submit proposals to me—and I was certain, agents and other editors—that lacked necessary information and were generally unprofessional.

Having recognized this problem, I followed the advice I so often give unpublished authors: Find a need and fill it.

In *The Fast-Track Course on How to Write a Nonfiction Book Proposal*, I have attempted to give abundant information in a sufficiently succinct, entertaining, and accessible manner that people will actually read and use. The publishing world has been in a state of flux for a few years now. In this second edition, I've attempted to address this moving target. For up-to-date information on where the digital age is taking book publishing, please visit my blog at TheWriteThought.com/blog.

• • •

There are too many people who helped with this book to thank each individually, but I especially want to acknowledge Dave Marion, a good friend, old-style gentleman, bon vivant, and one of the best editors I've known. I also would like to thank attorney/author Jonathan Kirsch for allowing me to include his model agency agreement and his model publishing agreement as appendixes to this book.

"This is a very important book. In fact, it's too important to publish."

First Things

TENS OF THOUSANDS OF ORDINARY PEOPLE, PEOPLE JUST LIKE YOU and me, will have their nonfiction books published this year. For many of them, this will be their first time to be published.

Hundreds of these men and women will write their books with lofty dreams of fame and fortune, expecting, or at least hoping, their books will become international best sellers—don't laugh, it does happen. Yet most of us write with more modest goals in mind:

- Many write to further their careers—published authors stand out as leaders in their respective fields.

- Some write to tell their life stories—well-written memoirs have been a hot genre since Mary Karr's best-selling *The Liars' Club* was published in 1995.

- Some write to further a cause—registered nurse Sally Pacholok wrote the internationally acclaimed *Could It Be B_{12}?* because she knew from experience that many doctors misdiagnose a B_{12} deficiency.

- Others want to record local history before it is forgotten—Catherine Morison Rehart has attracted national attention due to the success of her series of regional (Central California) history books, *The Valley's Legends & Legacies*.

- Others write because they have a bit of esoteric knowledge they want to share—*Been There, Should've Done That: 995 Tips for Making the Most of College*, by Suzette Tyler, has been in print since 1997.

- Some write to entertain—Simon Bond's *101 Uses for a Dead Cat* has been causing laughter and infuriating cat lovers since 1988.

- Some write to instruct—*How to Cheat at Gardening and Yard Work: Shameless Tricks for Growing Radically Simple Flowers, Veggies, Lawns, Landscaping, and More* by Jeff Bredenberg aims to simplify and speed up your outdoor chores.

- Some simply have a passion for their subject—physician Siddhartha Mukherjee's *The Emperor of All Maladies: A Biography of Cancer,* a *Publishers Weekly* best book of 2010, sold 84,000 hardcover copies in its first six months.

- Still others write to fulfill a need their inner muse causes to rise up in them.

Whatever your motivation, if you have the desire, the tenacity, and at least a modicum of writing skills, you too can join the ranks of published nonfiction book authors.

Your first step is to choose a topic.

Your second is to write a book proposal.

Sell your book to a publisher before you write it

Most nonfiction books are sold to a publishing house on the basis of a book proposal, usually before the book has been completely written—including books from first-time authors. This means you don't even have to write the book until you have in hand a contract and, in most cases, an advance against royalties.

A word about editors and agents

"Editor" is a title given to many people with various duties at a publishing house. The "managing editor's" duties, for instance, may have more to do with the day-to-day running of the business than reading and editing manuscripts. The editor in charge of acquiring manuscripts to publish often bears the title "acquisitions editor." At many houses, the lines between editorial duties are somewhat blurred, with editors sharing duties to one extent or another.

Literary agents function as the go-between for author and publisher. Two of the main functions of an agent are to sell a publisher on the idea of publishing an author's manuscript and to negotiate the best deal for the author.

(You approach a literary agent exactly the same way you approach an editor. As such, in order to make this book more readable, instead of writing "agent or editor" in each reference, I have simply used the term "editor." For this same reason I have dispensed with dual pronoun usages such as "his or hers.")

> **"Whatever your motivation, if you have the desire, the tenacity, and at least a modicum of writing skills, you too can join the ranks of published nonfiction book authors."**

What is a book proposal?

A book proposal is a ten- to fifty-page document designed to give an acquisitions editor enough information about your book and enough confidence in you as a writer that he will offer to publish it. The proposal must convince him that the book will sell enough copies to make a profit, in addition to returning the expense in time and money his publishing house will need to invest.

Factors an editor will consider are the book's topic and the public's interest in this topic, your qualifications to write this book, existing competition in the form of other similar books, and a host of elements that define his company's publishing program.

Since your book proposal stands the chance of being the last thing of yours an editor will read, it must be an example of your best writing.

I've already written my whole book, so I don't need a book proposal, right?

Wrong, for two reasons: Editors don't have the time to read whole manuscripts to find out if they are interested in a book, and a book proposal has information in it about market potential, competition, your qualifications, and other things that an editor needs to know in order to make a decision.

But stress not—writing a book proposal is a good drill to help you impartially evaluate your book. When you're done with the book proposal, you may find yourself going back and reworking parts of your book.

Writing a book proposal sounds like a lot of work. Won't the editor just see the brilliance of my idea and jump at it?

Books are sold to editors in many different ways, and a formal book proposal isn't always necessary—Dean Koontz could get a contract for a book on how to write scary stories with a phone call (Dean, if you're reading this, give me a call), as could O.J. Simpson for his memoirs—if he decided to confess and prison authorities allowed it.

Sometimes an author meets an editor socially, and a deal for a book ensues. Experts or other high-profile people are occasionally contacted by an editor in need of a book on a specific subject and a contract is signed without a formal book proposal being produced.

But, for those of us with average fame and average luck, the chances of selling an editor on a book project are increased immensely with a professional, well-thought-out, and well-organized book proposal.

How long should a book proposal be?

As the old saw about a woman's skirt goes, your proposal should be short enough to be interesting, but long enough to cover the subject. In most instances, a well-written proposal will run between ten and fifty pages.

Unlike with your high school English teacher, longer isn't better. You won't get extra points with an editor if you make him wade through five thousand unessential words. Be sure you include all necessary material, but, as is best in any writing, search out and expunge the superfluous.

Publishers as specialists

The large, primarily New York-based, publishers often publish across a spectrum of genres. But, like doctors or attorneys who specialize in one area of medicine or law, most publishers are specialists. One publisher might publish only spiritual titles, another only large-sized art books destined for coffee tables. Still another may only publish books on California subjects.

Independent publishers often concentrate on a tightly focused niche market, perhaps books for firefighters or books dealing with Miami-Dade County history.

Many agents also specialize, developing contacts and working only with editors interested in certain types of books.

> **"But, for those of us with average fame and average luck, the chances of selling an editor on a book project are increased immensely with a professional, well-thought-out, and well-organized book proposal."**

Conventional publishers

A conventional publisher will contract with you for certain rights to your work. These rights may include the right to publish your book in hardcover, paperback, mass-market paperback, electronic versions, or any combination thereof.

If yours is a book that has movie potential, dramatic rights may be included in the agreement. The publisher also may wish to obtain the right to license spin-off products, such as imprinted coffee mugs or calendars, or to publish, or to license others to publish, the book in a foreign language. The author typically shares in the revenue generated from these rights.

Any or all these rights may be limited geographically, say North American rights or British Commonwealth rights. (See "The Author's Bundle of Rights," page 107, for a more complete explanation of rights.)

Conventional publishers make their profit from the sale of your book and pay you royalties. Many pay an advance against future royalty earnings.

For the most part, conventional publishers are the only publishers that have open lines of distribution to libraries, chain stores, catalogs, independent bookstores, and other retailers, and are the only publishers that will market your book.

Agents will only approach conventional publishers.

Self-publishing

Technological advances have created a huge swell in the number of self-publishers, which in turn has made self-publishing more acceptable than it was a decade ago when I wrote the first edition of this book.

A self-publisher is an author who starts his own publishing company—complete with business licenses, UPS account, investment capital, an accounting system, and other requisites of doing business.

A self-publisher obtains his own ISBNs (the unique identifying number used with each edition of the book—you get them at ISBN.org), hires an editor and proofreader, works with a graphic designer, works with a book printer, and plans and executes his own marketing.

There are two main advantages to self-publishing. One is you have complete control over your book. This includes content, title, subtitle, and cover design. Another is that a self-publisher makes both the author's profit and the publisher's profit, if any.

Drawbacks include the fact that self-publishing requires an investment of time and money, both of which may prove to be ill-spent.

One of the best scenarios for self-publishing is when the author is a frequent public speaker and conducts back-of-the-room sales of his books at the places he speaks.

Self-publishing isn't for everyone. Most authors, today and, IMHO, long into the future will be best served partnering with a conventional publisher.

If you are considering self-publishing, read Dan Poynter's *The Self-Publishing Manual* before doing anything else. This is the book most often recommended to anyone new to the world of self-publishing—with cause.

Online publishers

What looks like a publisher, acts like a publisher, and sounds like a publisher, but isn't a publisher? A vanity press.

It is an old ploy. For decades, companies have masqueraded as publishers in an effort to fool authors into paying to have their books "published."

These businesses make their money off the payment the author gives them and, contrary to what their sales pitches may say, do little or no actual marketing of your book.

Old-style vanity presses charge you to design, print, and bind a number of copies of your book and either store them for you or ship them to you.

Operations similar in many ways have appeared on the Internet, utilizing technologies that allow a book to be set up to be printed one copy at a time—this is called "print-on-demand," or "POD."

Many of these operations provide services that format your book to be downloaded for reading on an e-book device like the iPad or Kindle.

Few, if any, copies originating from these operations actually find their way onto bookstore or other retailers' shelves and, while some of these books do become available through online bookstores such as Amazon.com, without a realistic marketing program behind each title, sales are likely to be feeble.

There are some instances when you may find these services to be of sufficient value to use. For instance, if you want a few copies for friends and family, or if your main plan for marketing your books is at seminars you present.

Some of the problems you may encounter when dealing with one of these operations include:

• Confusing terminology or the misuse of publishing terms. For example, one prominent print-on-demand company's ad reads: "Get broad distribution, affordable services and *high author royalties.*" (Italics mine.)

• Above market setup fees.

• Setup fees may include only one or two copies. Additional copies must be purchased at additional cost.

• Pressure to purchase additional add-on services.

• Pressure to purchase additional copies.

• Costly "marketing packages" that overpromise and under deliver. (One package offered to set up a book signing in a single warehouse club location for $4,000. I hope there were no takers.)

• Hidden charges and fees.

• An economic model that effectively rules out retailer participation.

If you plan on writing a check to a business that claims to be a publisher (remember, conventional publishers don't charge you, they pay you), calls itself a "subsidy publisher," or offers to help you "self-publish," do your due diligence and make sure you understand the value and limitations of what you are paying for.

Large corporation-owned publishers vs. smaller independent publishers

Inevitably, when I speak at writer's conferences, an author comes up and asks me if it would be better for her to look for a large conventional publisher or a smaller independent publisher.

I tell these authors I have no absolute answer to this question because each type of house has its strengths and weaknesses, as does each author and each book, and, besides, it's only with 20–20 hindsight that we will know for certain if the author chose correctly. Authors don't seem to find my reply very satisfying. Since you probably don't either, here are some things to consider:

₥Y WRITING SKILLS AREN'T SO GREAT.

Believe it or not, if you've got a solid idea, but are just a competent writer, you'll likely find a publisher. But, as you can imagine, the better the writing, the better your chances. Here are five things you can do to improve your writing:

• Read *The Elements of Style* by E. B. White and William Strunk, Jr.

• Join a writer's critique group where you'll critique others' works and they will critique yours. (Contact a local writer's club to find a critique group, or start your own.)

• Write a lot. Write for your office newsletter, write letters to family members, write a blog, write articles for the local giveaway newspapers you find at cafés and 7-11s, keep a journal. The key is to write nearly everyday.

• Read a lot. You'll never be a great writer until you're a great reader.

• Take a writing class at a local college or adult school.

Large publishers

• Large publishers often offer bigger advances. This is important if your book doesn't sell well because it will be the only money you'll receive.

• Large publishers usually command better distribution into the retailers than does an independent. This often translates into bigger sales. It also means your Aunt Ida has a better chance of finding your book in that quaint café-bookstore in Trenton.

• Large publishers expect an author to do much of the book's marketing and promotion.

• Large publishers are usually part of an even larger corporate conglomerate and as such have a reputation as impersonal and bureaucratic.

• Large publishers usually have a bigger promotion budget. If any publisher is going to pay for an enormous pile of your books to be at the front door of every Barnes and Noble superstore (you didn't think each store manager just picked which books to stack out there, did you?), it'll be a large publisher.

• Large houses are notorious for dropping all promotion for a title that is slow coming out of the gate.

• Being published by a large, well-known publisher affords the author greater bragging rights at cocktail parties.

Independent publishers

• Independents tend to be more successful with niche books than large publishers. This is because independents often focus on a single field, and their editors and marketing people become experts in this field. Niche magazines recognize these publishers and are anxious to review their books. Consumers begin to trust them and often loyally purchase their new titles.

• Independents have a reputation for keeping books in print longer. This gives the book a chance to find its audience. Some books don't take off until the second year after publication, or even later. That a book stays in print is particularly important to an author who plans to make back-of-the-room sales of her book at seminars or other presentations over a number of years.

• Independent publishers expect an author to do much of the book's marketing and promotion.

• Barnes and Noble reports that it gets most of its titles—if not most of its sales—from independents.

• Libraries, which constitute a large market for nonfiction books, are as willing to buy books published by independents as they are from the large publishers.

• Independent publishers are thought of as being more personal and caring. You often can call and talk to the owner of an independent if you have a problem. As an author, you'll probably mean more to an independent. (Of course, this relative closeness can backfire for a publisher. I have had one or two authors who thought nothing of calling me first thing every Monday to discuss something as urgent as the proper placement of a comma.)

> **"***Since your book proposal stands the chance of being the last thing of yours an editor will read, it must be an example of your best writing.***"**

• Independents often focus more heavily on nontraditional outlets for their books, such as gift shops, museums, and tourist attractions. Since these outlets tend to have a smaller, more focused selection of titles, a single title often enjoys larger sales than it would in a traditional bookstore. Another bonus is that these outlets often buy on a nonreturnable basis, whereas books sold into the traditional book market generally are sold on terms that allow their return to the publisher if the retailer doesn't sell them. (This affects the author because publishers don't pay royalties on returned books.)

• Independents will often continue to market a title that starts off with slow sales.

• Independent publishers often offer the same royalties as larger houses. This helps to counter receipt of a smaller advance, particularly if an independent keeps a book in print longer than a large publisher would have.

So, what's the bottom line? At least for your first book, you are probably not going to get a choice of publishers. When an offer comes, check to be certain that the publisher is reputable and that the contract is fair, and then take a leap of faith.

Will I need an agent?

With most independent publishing companies and some of the bigger houses, you won't require the services of a literary agent in submitting your proposal. However, a good agent will not only have her submissions moved to the top of the editor's slush pile, she will act as your business advisor and career counselor, easily earning her 15 percent commission.

One of the valuable things an agent may do is review your book proposal with an eye to having you make it stronger before it is sent to a publisher. This alone may be worth the agent's commission, since a weak proposal is less likely to make the sale to the editor.

Agents are often reluctant to spend time submitting to independent publishers because these smaller houses share a reputation for offering modest advances and paying less in royalties. However, with the large houses paying less today, and some of the smaller ones paying more, this distinction is becoming somewhat diminished.

If you decide to use an agent, your agreement might state that she has a certain number of months to present your proposal to the larger houses, and if something isn't brewing by the end of this time period, you are free to begin submitting the proposal to the independents without incurring any obligation to the agent if you are successful.

If your genre of book is only published by independents—some topics are too esoteric to attract a large house—you might arrange for an agent to review both your book proposal and any resulting contract offers on a set-fee basis.

Remember, you use the same proposal and submission process to attract an agent's interest as you do an editor's. As mentioned above, the advice in this book for approaching and working with an editor applies equally to agents.

How do I find the right publisher or agent to submit to?

Since it is a waste of time to submit to publishing houses or literary agencies that would not be interested in the type of book you're writing, it is important to learn what type of material an agent or a publisher would like to see before submitting.

There are a number of good guides to publishers and agents on the market. Most can be found at a decent public library. *Writer's Market* is quite good and probably the best known. *Literary Market Place* (*LMP*) supplies information on publishers as well as a host of other industry entities. *LMP* is a big, multivolume work that may be found in most public libraries. *The International Directory of Little Magazines and Small Presses* has the most comprehensive listing of smaller, independent presses, which are often overlooked by authors (Read: aren't inundated each year by hundreds of book proposals).

> **"At least on your first book, you are probably not going to get a choice of publishers. When an offer comes, check to be certain that the publisher is reputable and that the contract is fair, and then take a leap of faith."**

The best of guides to publishers and agents give the name of the publisher or agent and delineate what types of material each publishes or is interested in seeing. They also give the name of the person you should submit to, how to contact this person—e-mail, snail mail, with query only, or full proposal—and if he or she wishes to see multiple submissions, that is, submissions sent to more than one agent or editor at a time.

Another way to find a publisher is to visit a large bookstore and look for books similar to the one you want to write. Publishers of similar books are good candidates to approach with your book idea. Look these publishers up in the guides mentioned above to obtain editors' names and addresses.

Editors change jobs and publishing companies move. Spend the price of a phone call to check that you are submitting to the correct person at the correct address. It is the mark of an amateur to address a query letter or proposal to an editor's predecessor.

SASE

Because of the volume of submissions editors receive each year, it is customary for an author, when submitting via snail mail, to include with a query letter or a proposal a self-addressed, stamped envelope for the editor to use when responding. Undoubtedly, an editor who is interested in your book project will contact you whether you have included an SASE or not. Thus, an SASE's primary purpose is so you'll hear from the editor if he isn't interested.

The SASE that you send with your proposal can be a #10 business envelope (in which case, the editor will trash or recycle the material you sent), but I suggest you include a large envelope with enough postage to get back everything you send. Editors have been known to make notations on rejected proposals that may prove helpful to you.

Do not send money, a check, or loose stamps in the place of an SASE.

Multiple submissions: smart or taboo?

Some agents and editors ask that you don't submit your proposal to anyone else until they have had a chance to respond. They do this because they don't want to take the time to consider your proposal and then find out it is no longer available because another agency or publishing house has picked it up.

It's a fact of life that editors usually take one to three months—and sometimes longer—to respond to an unsolicited book proposal or query letter. It is also a fact of life that book proposals must often be presented to dozens of publishers before finding a home. You do the math. Can an author afford single submissions? Perhaps...if she hasn't reached her seventh birthday yet.

Do you notify the editor that yours is a multiple submission? You can; it's polite. Many authors indicate this by placing "simultaneous submission" at the bottom of the last page of the query. Some even feel this is subtle pressure to get the editor to hurry and make a decision. Just remember, the easiest and quickest decision an editor can make is to say "No." Do you really want to rush him?

If you decide to multiple submit, should you submit to an editor whose listings in the guides say "No multiple submissions accepted"? Sure. In some instances, the editor receiving the proposal doesn't even know the listings say that, and, of course, if it's a work he would like to publish, he's not going to decline to consider it because of a technicality.

What's a query letter?

A query letter is a letter you send to an agent or an editor asking if he would like to see a full proposal on your book idea. Rarely should a query letter be longer than six to eight paragraphs. See page 27 for more information about query letters.

Mettee's secret

Shhhssh! Don't tell anyone. It's a secret I reveal only at writer's conferences—it helps draw a crowd to my workshops if a rumor gets out I'm telling secrets—and even then I make the participants swear a blood oath to never tell another soul. But, since you bought this book, I'll share it with you. It's this:

> Always send your full book proposal with your query letter—even if the publisher's listing in the guides says "Query first only."

Pretty heady stuff, huh? Okay, well, I didn't say it was an earth-shattering secret. But if you adhere to it, you'll sell more books.

Why? Let's take a look at the options an editor has when he gets a query. First, if he hates the idea, he'll reject it immediately. On the other hand, if he loves the idea, he'll immediately request to see the full proposal.

But what if he's a fence-sitter? What if he's thinking "Well, this is a pretty good idea. Maybe I should ask for the whole proposal...

but..."? The next thing that goes through his mind is, he's really busy and if he asks to see a proposal, he's morally obligated to remember he asked for it and to bring it to the top of the slush pile and to read it, and if he doesn't like it, to respond with more than a form rejection letter, and the author might actually phone to talk about it, and does he have time for all this for a book he's not really excited about?

> **"** *...If you decide to multiple submit, should you submit to an editor whose listings in the guides say 'No multiple submissions accepted'? Sure.* **"**

Or the marketing department might call looking for those prepublication blurbs he'd promised them, or his boss might come in for a short chat or to drop off those new budget figures the editor's supposed to go over—by tomorrow morning. In these instances, he's too likely to do the easy thing, to pull out that little slip of paper that begins "Thank you for letting us see this...."

But, if the sheet right beneath your query is the first page of your proposal, you have a second chance to hook him. And do you think for a minute, if he likes it, he'll reject the proposal because you broke the rules and included it with the query? Naw. Won't happen. Not on this green earth.

But remember, it's our little secret. Don't tell anyone. Promise?

How long should I wait to hear from an editor?

It must have been different in the years before World War II. The famous Scribner and Son's editor Max Perkins apparently dropped whatever his plans were on days new material arrived from then relatively unknown authors such as Hemingway and Fitzgerald. Unfortunately, today's acquisition editors support the leaden burden of workloads that extend well beyond reading the incoming mail.

They attend marketing meetings, budget meetings, title selection meetings, work with authors already on contract, analyze data, write reports, and even occasionally do some editing. An editor may not get to your proposal for six to eight weeks—or longer. And, while the majority of editors are sensitive to an author's wish for a quick response, most do not relish calls from authors checking up on a proposal's status.

Here's what you should do:

• Figure no news is good news. When the editor opens your proposal, he has two choices: return it immediately with the dreaded "...does not fit into our publishing program at this time" or set it aside while he thinks about it. In larger houses, even if he loves your project, it still has to pass the editorial committee, which may only meet once a month. Be patient.

• After sixty days, you might send a self-addressed, stamped postcard with a note inquiring about the proposal's progress. On the message side of the postcard, list the following with places the editor can make a check mark:

_____ We have no record of receiving your proposal. Please resubmit.

_____ It's in the slush pile working its way to the top. We'll get to it as soon as we can.

_____ Thanks, but it didn't work for us, so we returned it. You should get it any day now.

_____ It has been read and is under consideration.

A similar e-mail might do the trick if you submitted via e-mail.

But I get antsy checking an empty mailbox everyday.

We all have this kid-on-Christmas-Eve syndrome to one degree or another, and, like with a kid at Christmastime, this anticipation can be part of the fun.

WHY DIDN'T THEY LIKE IT? IT MUST BE A BUM IDEA.

There are many reasons a publishing company turns down a project that have little or nothing to do with the quality of the proposal or the salability of the book.

If you get a generic rejection such as "Thank you for submitting your proposal, but it doesn't work with us at this time," don't be discouraged. It *may* be that the editor just doesn't want to offend you by telling you how awful he thinks your proposal is, but this isn't necessarily the case. Editors are often reluctant to give you a concrete reason for declining your book for at least four other reasons:

- It takes time out of an already too-busy day.

- Giving a reason suggests that the door is still open and appears to the author as an opportunity to begin a dialogue with the editor when, if he wanted to discuss your fixing or changing something and resubmitting the proposal, he would have said so.

- They don't have the time or desire to explain how elements particular to their company's publishing program came into play to nix your project.

- They know they aren't the final authority on what will or won't work with an ever-changing public—every editor who has spent much time in the acquisitional trenches has a story to tell about the successful book he declined—and they don't want to discourage you.

It is important, when dwelling on the fate of your submission, that you don't conjure up evil characteristics for the editors who, in reality, haven't singled you out to ignore and frustrate. Thoughts such as these are guaranteed to lead to hard feelings, despair, and discouragement.

A better strategy is to be working on another writing project in the meantime. Use the research you did to write your proposal to write an article and submit it to an appropriate magazine, or develop another, completely different book idea and begin work on the proposal for that one. You'd be surprised how having a second iron in the fire reduces the anxiety about the first.

How are royalties figured?

Royalties, the money a publisher pays an author for the right to publish her book, are figured on the number of copies sold by the publisher, less any copies returned to the publisher—yes, even e-books can get returned.

Often a contract will call for royalties to be paid as a percentage of the book's cover price.

Another way royalties may be figured is as a percentage of the net amount a publisher receives for its sales of a book. In the book trade, a publisher sells to various wholesale and retail accounts at discounted prices to allow these accounts to resell the book at a profit.

A publisher might give a wholesaler a 55 percent discount. Or, to put it another way, the publisher would charge the wholesaler 45 percent of the cover price. In this case, on a $20 book, a 10 percent royalty paid on the net amount received by a publisher would earn an author $.90 per book [$20 x .45 = $9.00 x .10 = $.90]. This works out to be 4½ percent of the cover price. With a contract that calls for royalties to be figured as 10 percent of the cover price, the author would earn $2.00 per book. Be sure you understand how, according to the contract you sign, your publisher will figure royalties.

So what's fair? Sans extraordinary circumstances, the royalties you contract for with a large publisher should fall somewhere near the following figures. Economics often force smaller publishing houses to offer somewhat less for the first 5,000 to 10,000 copies sold. The royalty rates below are shown as a percentage of the cover price. To be comparable, royalty percents figured on the net amount received by the publisher would need to be approximately twice those listed.

Hardcover Nonfiction

First 5,000	5–10%
Next 5,000	10–15%
Thereafter	10–15%

Trade Paperback Nonfiction

First 10,000	5–10%
Thereafter	8–15%

At this writing, e-book royalties are still in flux. This is due in part to the uncertainty in how the e-book pie will be cut up among the various stakeholders, including publishers, distributors, data depositories, and retailers. It is a brand new world out there!

Today, e-book royalties range from a low of about 20 percent to a high of about 50 percent of net revenues. If the publisher offers you something on the low end of this scale, the Author's Guild suggests you ask for the right to renegotiate in, say, two years.

Unlike genre novels, it is exceedingly rare for a nonfiction book to be published in a mass-market format before being released in a hardcover or trade paperback edition, but royalties for mass-market editions are usually slightly lower than those for trade paperback.

Royalties also include the author's share of the monies a publisher receives when it licenses subsidiary rights, such as the right to publish the book in a foreign language, to a third party.

What is an advance?

An advance is an amount paid to an author *against* future royalty earnings. It is customary for an advance to be paid one-half upon the signing of a contract and one-half upon receipt by the publisher of an acceptable manuscript, although any formula a publisher and an author agree upon can be used.

An advance is deducted from the royalties a book earns before any further payment is made to the author. If sales of a book are sufficient that the royalties earned equal or exceed the amount of the advance, the book is said to have "earned out its advance." Under most circumstances, if the author delivers to the publisher an acceptable manuscript, the advance is not refundable to the publisher, and, on books that don't sell well, the advance becomes the only money an author receives.

Both publishers and authors like to see an advance earned out: the author because she now begins to find regular royalty checks in her mailbox, checks that will continue to arrive until the book stops selling, and the publisher because its sales projections at the beginning of the project have proven to be correct.

Normally, it is only after an advance has been earned out that publisher and author alike begin to make significant money on a book.

What kind of an advance should I expect?

There's no absolute answer to this question. Some say it should be equal to the royalties that would be earned if the publisher's initial press run sold out. Thus, if a publisher planned a first printing of 5,000 copies and your contract called for a $2.00 per book royalty, your advance would be $10,000. But other factors often come into play.

Foremost among these factors is the author's publishing history. Sebastian Junger, author of *The Perfect Storm* and other *New York Times* best sellers, is in an excellent position to command a large advance. A first time author is not.

Traditionally, part of the advance is intended to cover expenses an author may incur because she is writing the book. If extensive travel is involved or funds are needed to acquire permissions to use copyrighted material, the advance may need to be adjusted accordingly.

For years there's been a tendency for large publishers to give celebrities giant advances, which works out well if you happen to be the celebrity, but limits the amount these publishers can pay to other authors.

Independent publishers and university publishers may offer no advance or only a token one.

The following figures, from a survey of authors' advances conducted by the National Writer's Union, illustrates the large variances one encounters when trying to tie down how much an advance should be:

Nonfiction Hardcover: $5,000 to $150,000

Nonfiction Softcover: $1,000 to $100,000

In the end, it comes down to what the publisher feels it can afford and what the author is willing to accept. I have had authors tell me they would need enough money to live on for the year or so it would take them to write their book. Since none of these authors resided in a cave subsisting on wild berries, I was forced to decline.

When I get a sale, should I have an attorney look at the contract?

It is always safest to have a professional go over any contract before you sign it. Reputable publishers will not object to this. If you choose to have an attorney take a look at a publishing contract, be certain you have selected an attorney specializing in intellectual property law.

If you have an agent, an essential part of her job is to make sure your contract is up to snuff. For a set fee, many agents will read a contract and advise an author whom they are not formally representing.

Kirsch's Handbook of Publishing Law, by Jonathan Kirsch, is an excellent resource for authors who want to better understand their own contracts and the process of contracting.

The dreaded rejection slip

No writer worth her thesaurus hasn't collected a stack of rejection letters. Don't become discouraged until you have exhausted the list of potential publishers for books like yours.

It isn't rare for a proposal to go out fifty to sixty times before being picked up by a publisher. I once bought a book—*The New Baby Owner's Manual: The Care and Fine-Tuning of Your New Baby* by Horst D. Weinberg, M.D.—that had been turned down by forty-six publishers. The forty-eighth potential publisher (the good doctor was a believer in multiple submissions) also made an offer for it. Eventually, we translated it into Spanish for the North American Hispanic market and later sold Mexican and South American rights to a Mexican publisher, Selector Publishing. A year later, we signed a contract with Shanghai Popular Science Press in the People's Republic of China, which published a Chinese language edition marketed in much of Asia. Today, *The New Baby Owner's Manual* is available to billions of people on three continents. What if Dr. Weinberg had become discouraged after receiving ten, twenty, thirty, or forty rejections?

After you have fine-tuned your proposal and had a professional freelance editor go over it for content as well as grammar and spelling—you can find these people in ads in the back of writing magazines, by networking with a local writer's group, or by calling your city newspaper and asking for a referral from someone at the editorial desk—put it out to twenty to thirty agents and/or publishers and see if it floats. Make changes to your proposal only if you find you are getting the same negative feedback from more than one trusted source. (By the way, I understand the catch-22 inherent here. Since most editors don't give you a substantial reason when rejecting your idea, how are you to collect enough feedback to decide if you need to adjust your proposal? One good way is to attend a writer's conference—you can find one in your area by checking WRITING.SHAWGUIDES.COM on the Internet. Most conferences allow attendees to meet and discuss their book ideas face-to-face with agents and editors.)

Copyright

Authors are often both concerned and confused about copyright laws. Below are some copyright basics in the United States. (If you are writing for publication in another country, research that country's copyright laws.)

- You don't have to register your work with the federal government to obtain copyright protection. Copyright begins automatically as soon as a work is "fixed in a tangible medium of expression." For a writer, this means as soon as what you write is put on paper, audiotape, computer disk, or other reproducible form.

> **"No writer worth her thesaurus hasn't collected a stack of rejection letters. Don't become discouraged until you have exhausted the list of potential publishers for books like yours."**

- Some additional benefits are gained when the copyright mark (©) and the copyright owner's name and the date of copyright are placed on the material, as well as when it is registered with the Copyright Office (COPYRIGHT.GOV). For instance, if the work is registered within three months of publication, the copyright owner maintains the right to collect attorney's fees and certain statutory damage amounts from infringers without having to prove monetary harm.

- It is common practice for a publisher to obtain copyright registration in the author's name after the book is published.

- As a practical matter, agents, editors, and others in the publishing industry rarely steal written material.

- Ideas themselves are not copyrightable, only original, expressive work is copyrightable.

One of the concerns authors have is how much of another's work they can use without infringing on that person's copyright. This is truly a gray area. Under the "fair use" doctrine of the Copyright Act, use of "a copyrighted work...for purposes such as criticism, comment, news reporting, teaching, scholarship, or research is not an infringement of copyright."

Since this wording is less than precise, the courts have historically looked at four factors in making their determination:

- the purpose of the use

- the nature of the copyrighted work

- the portion of the work used

- the effect of this use upon the market for the copyrighted work.

To get a feeling for what falls under the fair use doctrine, watch for quoted material in books that you read and check the "acknowledgments" or "permissions" page to see if permission to use the material is listed.

When in doubt about what constitutes fair use of copyrighted material, obtain permission.

For a more complete, yet concise, summary of copyrights, read the chapter "Copyright: What Every Author Should Know," by John D. Zelezny, in *The Portable Writers' Conference*, edited by yours truly.

"We're reducing your royalties by ten percent due to spelling errors."

The Query Letter

The goal

THE JOB OF A QUERY LETTER IS TO GET AN EDITOR OR AGENT TO ASK to see your full proposal.

The format

A query letter is a business letter. As such, it takes the form of a business letter.

Single space query letters. Put your book's working title in all caps or italicize it. Use a business typeface such as Times New Roman. Never is it cute or quaint to use a decorative or script typeface in the body of your query letter.

It is fine to use business stationery from your job, and it's all to the better if your work is related to the subject of your book.

If you don't have a business letterhead you want to use, use a personal letterhead. Today, with computers, you don't even have to pay to have your letterhead printed. Using your word processing program, you can simply center your name and contact information—here a decorative font is fine—at the top of your letter. Softly colored paper—not the fluorescent hues—is appropriate, but not necessary.

Some beginning writers feel that placing a title such as "Writer" on their personal letterhead gives them validity. I suggest you shy away from listing yourself as a writer unless you have the credentials (numerous publications) to back it up. Without the credentials, it just comes off as hokey.

Address your letter to an individual by name. Never use "Dear Editor" or "To whom it may concern." Get the name from the guides listed on page 110, but be sure to call to verify that this person is still the correct person to receive submissions. If you are unsure of what honorific—Miss, Mrs., Dr., etc.—you should use, ask for this information also.

Triple check that you have spelled the editor's or agent's name correctly before mailing your query.

Keep it short

Make your query succinct and to the point. Try to employ a high ratio of ideas to words. A query should rarely be more than two pages in length.

The lead

The first paragraph or two of your query is called the lead. While nothing in your short letter to the editor is unimportant, the lead is the most important.

I once got a query that started out:

> I have written a 70,000-word manuscript which has taken me six years to complete.

In this case, the author has wasted the valuable lead by providing me with information I don't need to know—at least not right away. Yes, at some point, if I'm intrigued by the project, I'll need to know the anticipated word count, but I don't suppose I'll ever need to know that the guy's a slow writer.

Or sometimes the author begins by apologizing for the silliness of having written to me:

> Everybody in my family and all my friends have insisted that I search for a publisher to publish the book I plan on writing. It is only because of their insistence that I contact you.

A lead serves the same purpose as a sharp tug on a rod when fishing; it sets the hook. (Actually, the lead is sometimes referred to as the "hook.")

A good lead gets the editor interested. A truly righteous lead grabs him by the throat and doesn't let him go.

A good lead might start out with an anecdote:

> In her fifty-fifth year, divorcee Jane Montgomery, suffering from a severe case of empty-nest syndrome, found herself searching for a seemingly ever-elusive something that would make her life meaningful. Twice Cleveland paramedics revived her from a self-inflicted overdose of prescription drugs. Today, barely three years later, Sister Jane ministers to the poor and disenfranchised in Tijuana, Mexico, as a member of an exclusive order of middle-aged nuns founded by an ex-Vietnam mercenary.

Or with a question:

> What do large vats of warm chicken fat, Bill Clinton, and *O, the Oprah Magazine* have in common?

Or with a statistic that points to a large population that will be interested in the book:

> Last year, 740,000 people in the United States were diagnosed with Malcolm's toe, an insidious and normally deadly disease that can be cured by following my simple regime of herbal teas and daily vinegar baths.

A well-phrased appeal to the editor's avarice might even work. One of the most eye-catching queries I've ever received started something like this:

> I have a purchase order, from a large insurance company, for 25,000 copies of my proposed book.

While I admit to these examples being a bit fanciful, the point is, the lead needs to pique the interest of the editor so as to draw him into the rest of the query and, eventually, into asking to see the complete proposal.

The high concept

The high concept—sometimes called the "elevator speech" because it needs to be short enough to deliver between floors in the fortuitous event that you find yourself in an elevator with an editor, agent, reviewer, reporter, movie producer, or some other exalted personage—is the gist of your book distilled into one or two sentences. This usually will take a bit of thought, but it is certainly worth the effort.

> **"While nothing in your short letter to the editor is unimportant, the lead is the most important."**

Often, when I ask an author what her book will be about, she launches into a lengthy explanation that starts off with an incident in her childhood, which leads her to recount experiences she had in college, before she segues to her middle-aged endeavors which, all combined, awakened this passion for whatever it is she's writing about.

Eventually she'll tell me the subject of the book, but I still won't have any clear idea where her book will take the reader. And, of course, by then, I may have fallen asleep.

What I really wanted to hear was a one- or two-sentence capsulation of the essence of her book, like this one for a book titled *Long Distance Grandparenting*:

> My book is about the positive effect good grandparenting can have on children, even though the grandparents live in a distant city, and it details strategies on how to achieve this. *Long Distance Grandparenting* will fill the need for grandparents who wish to be a stable part of their grandchildren's lives even in today's mobile society.

One effective way to communicate a high concept is to compare your book to another. For example, if you plan to write a book for people over 40 who are interested in learning to network with others, you might say your book will be the *How to Win Friends and Influence People* for the baby boomer generation. This technique not only relates your concept to a known factor, it psychologically associates it with a proven best seller.

One of the most intriguing high concept pitches I've heard (ironically, for a book that was never actually presented to me) came from a man I met at a writer's conference:

Think of my book as Dave Berry meets Yoda.

An editor who wants to publish your book will use this same high concept description to get the other decision makers in his company interested. After your book is published, the high concept will be used by salesmen presenting your title to bookstore buyers, and it will often find its way into catalog descriptions, press releases, and brochures.

In your query letter, the high concept may be used as your lead or follow closely after your lead.

Suggest a snappy title and descriptive subtitle

High up in your query, mention your book's title.

Nonfiction book titles are usually composed of two parts, the title and the subtitle.

Spend time formulating your title. A great title is often the thing that captures an editor's attention, because he knows a great title will sell a bunch of books.

The best titles are descriptive, colorful, intriguing, spirited, thought-provoking, and make an implied promise. The worst titles are vague and insipid.

If you study best-selling nonfiction books, you'll discover that many of them have catchy or memorable short titles combined with longer descriptive subtitles. We followed that premise when we named Betty Fielding's book *The Memory Manual: 10 Simple Things*

You Can Do to Improve Your Memory After 50. The implied promise is that, if you read *The Memory Manual,* you'll be less forgetful.

Here are some other successful titles and subtitles to get you thinking:

- *Baby Signs: How to Talk to Your Baby Before Your Baby Can Talk*

- *Breaking the Rules: Last Ditch Tactics for Landing the Man of Your Dreams*

- *Anatomy of the Spirit: The Seven Stages of Power and Healing*

- *Jesus CEO: Using Ancient Wisdom for Visionary Leadership*

- *Smart Love: The Compassionate Alternative to Discipline That Will Make You a Better Parent and Your Child a Better Person*

- *Starting on a Shoestring: Building a Business Without a Bankroll*

- *Galileo's Daughter: A Historical Memoir of Science, Faith and Love*

- *Answers to Satisfy the Soul: Clear, Straight Answers to 20 of Life's Most Perplexing Questions*

- *When Elephants Weep: The Emotional Lives of Animals*

- *Write Your Book Now! A Proven System to Start and FINISH the Book You've Always Wanted to Write!*

A title doesn't have to have two parts to be successful. Some are simply descriptive:

- *How to Live with a Neurotic Dog*

- *A Woman's Guide to Tantra Yoga*

- *How to Clean Practically Anything*

- *The Physics of Star Trek*

Other titles tout how comprehensive they are:

- *The Complete Book of Bread Machine Baking*
- *The Complete Book of Essential Oils and Aroma Therapy*
- *500 Beauty Solutions*
- *1001 Ways to Market Your Books*
- *1001 Sex Secrets Every Woman Should Know*
- *Encyclopedia of Natural Medicine*

WHAT MAKES A BEST SELLER?

Exceptions abound, but the best-selling nonfiction books, those that top the lists for years, tend to:

- deal with one or more of the Big Seven subjects: money, diet, health and fitness, beauty, romance, sex, and power
- be a blend of self-help and philosophy
- offer instruction or information that has the potential to change, to one degree or another, the life of the reader
- be written in a warm, positive, helpful voice
- use real-life anecdotes and quote real people
- contain a bit of humor.

Not all books can, or even should, embody each and every one of these qualities, but regardless of your subject or your intended audience, as you plan and write your book, keep these elements in mind.

Why this editor?

If you are using the shotgun approach to querying—which will be time-consuming and less effective—skip this step. But if you have selected an editor or his publishing company for a particular reason, explain why. Does his company produce a series—such as Quill Driver Books' Best Half of Life series for people over 50 or Wiley's Dummies series—into which your book will fit snugly? Or perhaps you are aware that this editor is passionate about your book's topic and has worked on comparable books.

Taking your query to this level of personalization will impress an editor and make your query stand out.

The synopsis

After you've got the editor's attention with your lead, introduced the title, presented your high concept, and told him why you are approaching him in particular, spend three to six paragraphs describing your book. Explain the material you will cover and in what style. What main points will your book address? Will you focus on a small facet of a subject or cover the topic broadly? Will you interview specialists and quote them? Give step-by-step instructions? Include anecdotes or lists? Will the writing be lighthearted but thoughtful? What illustrations will be used? Will your book be written for the novice or the expert?

In this section, tell why your approach is fresh or superior when compared to like titles on the market. If you are breaking new ground, say so. Point out if your book is particularly timely. The popularity of PBS's *Antique Roadshow* created a renewed interest in antiques and, in turn, a new hot market for books on collecting antiques.

Mention an approximate word count. (See page 56.) If this is to be the first book in a series, explain a bit about the other potential titles.

Who will buy it?

Include a paragraph on the size and makeup of the pool of likely buyers for your book. Identify any appropriate demographics,

Develop Your Platform While You Write

An author's "platform" is anything she brings to the table that helps sell her book. Most authors' platforms are made up of multiple items. A platform may include big, important things, like being elected to the Senate or hosting a national TV show. Authorship of a syndicated column is often a good platform. The column by Peter H. Gott, M.D. appears daily in 350 newspapers. When he mentions one of his books in the column, sales soar.

Being famous is a platform in itself. When we contracted with Dr. Ruth K. Westheimer to publish *Dr. Ruth's Sex After 50*, we knew Dr. Ruth's international celebrity status would help sell the book.

Unfortunately, few of us are Senators, host TV shows, are internationally famous, or write syndicated columns. But we can do things such as developing a hefty schedule of speaking engagements—even if only in our local geographical area—or establishing ourselves as an authority in a particular industry by writing for trade periodicals and presenting at conferences.

One of the easiest things to do to promote yourself and your book is to create a noted online presence. A good guide to help you with this is *The Author's Guide to Building an Online Platform* by Stephanie Chandler. Another useful guide is Deltina Hay's *The Social Media Survival Guide*. (Full disclosure: Both are published by Quill Driver Books.)

Here are some things to consider:

- Build a website around yourself as an expert.
- Schedule public speaking engagements.
- Produce seminars.
- Blog.

- Comment on others' blogs.

- Write a magazine or newspaper column.

- Network with opinion makers who will talk up your book.

- Offer to appear at fundraisers, where partial proceeds from sales from your book can go to the nonprofit organization.

- Run naked down Fifth Avenue.

- Hold an annual contest.

- Watch for news on your subject, then call a reporter and offer to help with inside information.

- Issue press releases.

- Make videos, place them on your website, on YouTube, and use them in e-press releases.

If you don't have a platform already, start building yours today. If you do have one, see what you can do to enhance it before your book lands.

including age, gender, income level, or special interests shared by this group. Provide statistics showing how large this group is. (See page 46 for ideas on how to present the size of your potential market.)

Try to name at least two groups of potential buyers. For *The Pediatrician's New Baby Owner's Manual: Your Guide to the Care and Fine-Tuning of Your New Baby,* by Horst D. Weinberg, M.D., these groups included new parents themselves, grandparents and friends who would buy the book as a gift, health-care organizations which would purchase the book in bulk quantities to supply to their clients, and libraries.

Willingness to help market your book

It often comes as a surprise to new authors, but publishers, both small and large, are going to expect you to do much of the marketing of your book. Include here a short paragraph about your platform and what you can and will do to help your book sell. This might include blogging, funding your own five-city book tour, writing articles for publication, locating radio and TV shows willing to interview you, or presenting at seminars. The more, the better.

Express enthusiasm

Somewhere in the query you need to reveal your passion for your book and its subject. This may be done in the short bio you'll include or, better yet, demonstrate this passion in the paragraphs you use to describe the project.

Prepublication endorsements and foreword

If you can obtain an endorsement for the book or a foreword to the book from a prominent person in the book's field, mention it. For more on this, see page 52.

Your bio

Include a paragraph or two about yourself and why you're the one to write this book. This isn't the place for unbridled bragging, but it also isn't the place for abject modesty.

Mention books or articles you have had published or writing awards you've received. If your previous books have reached uncommon sales heights or your article publishing credits include big name periodicals, don't keep this a secret from the editor. If, on the other hand, you have no publishing credits, don't say so—just don't broach the subject.

Whether you've been published or not, list your credentials for writing this book. Do you hold a college degree or have years of experience applicable to the book's subject? Are you the one who single-handedly stopped the runaway train or nabbed the serial killer? Perhaps you conduct seminars for others in your industry or appear in infomercials. Do the courts call on you for expert testimony?

If none of these or similar qualifications apply, explain how you plan to research your topic—who you'll interview and what sources you'll consult.

An accomplishment that does not pertain to the book shouldn't be included unless it is extraordinary. For instance, you might want to mention that you are the ex-governor of Kentucky or hold the world land-speed record, even if neither of these have anything to do with the topic of your book, but you wouldn't want to mention that you've won your city-county golf tournament two years running unless this is somehow relevant.

> **"***It often comes as a surprise to new authors, but publishers, both small and large, are going to expect you to do much of the marketing of your book.***"**

Some don'ts

Nowhere in your query letter should you:

• bring up the subject of how much (or little) money you want

• mention an idea you have for another book, unless it will be part of a series with this one

• point out you are an unpublished author

• mention copyrighting

• beg or act desperate

• ask for advice or criticism

• say your mother (best friend, local librarian, bartender) loves the book

• predict best-sellerdom

- fawn

- guess at facts

- complain about another publisher turning you down

- include your complete job resumé

- claim it will be a book for everyone

- suggest the editor hurry or some other editor will beat him to it

- lie.

The close

Unless you choose to include your proposal with your query letter—as I advise, see page 15—mention in the last paragraph that you have a full proposal ready and would be delighted to send it. In either case, say you look forward to hearing from him, creating a subtle hint that you expect a response.

If you're using snail mail, after your signature and a blank line or two, type:

Encl.: SASE

to let the editor know you have enclosed a self-addressed, stamped envelope for his reply.

The Proposal

The goal

THE GOAL OF A BOOK PROPOSAL IS TO GET AN EDITOR TO AGREE TO publish your book.

The parts

Your proposal should have five parts:

1. The synopsis
2. A table of contents, including front and back matter
3. A chapter-by-chapter outline
4. Sample chapters
5. Supporting material

The synopsis

The first pages of your proposal—sometimes called the overview, outline, or introduction—are where you sell an editor on the idea of publishing your book.

In this synopsis, you tell the editor what your book is about, who's likely to buy it, and why. You furnish a one- or two-sentence high-concept description of the book. You explain what style you'll write it in and tell about charts, anecdotes, sidebars, or other special features you'll include. You list competing books and tell why yours will be better or different. You tell why you're the one to write it, how long it'll take you to finish it, what resources, if any, you'll need, and how you'll help to market it.

By the time an editor finishes reading this portion of the proposal, he should have a clear, complete concept of the project. If he likes it, the rest of the proposal only serves to prove to him that you can pull it off.

> **"While others counsel an author not to use the same lead she used in her query letter, I find using the same lead is usually best."**

Following is a description of the various parts of the synopsis. I have listed these parts in the order you would normally place them in your proposal, but, with the exception of the lead, the order may be changed and the parts may be blended together to fit your project or your style.

Not all successful proposals include all of these elements, but an author who eliminates too many of them does so at the peril of losing the sale. There is a checklist on page 105 for your use in making sure your proposal covers all the bases.

The lead

Go back to page 28 and reread the tips about writing a lead. While others counsel an author not to use the same lead she used in her query letter, I find using the same lead is usually best. Why? Well, as clever as I'm sure you are, one lead is inevitably going to be your stronger, so then the question arises, where do you put a weaker one? Should you put it in the query letter, which is the first and maybe the last thing an editor will look at? Or should you put it in the proposal, which may be read long after the editor has forgotten the brilliance of your query? And what if the editor passes the proposal, sans query letter, on to other decision makers in the publishing house?

It's unlikely the editor will tire of reading your lead, and the repetition may even serve to solidify the book's concept in his mind. Go with the most powerful lead you can write and use it both places.

Your book's title and subtitle

As discussed on page 31, the title and subtitle you suggest for your book is of primary importance. Place something like "Proposal for *Your Title: Your Subtitle*" on the first page of your proposal (see page 106), then mention it early in the body of your proposal.

The high concept

This is the same succinct, one- or two-sentence description of your book you used in your query letter (see page 30). The high concept may be the first part of your lead, embedded elsewhere in your lead, or it may closely follow your lead. It often works well to include the high concept immediately after the first mention of your title and subtitle. Here's an example for an imaginary book:

> *The Life and Times of the White-Bearded Gnu: My Days Running with the Wildebeests* may be thought of as a combination of *Robinson Crusoe* and *Born Free*.

The meat

Are you old enough to remember that Wendy's TV commercial with the spunky old lady asking, "Where's the beef?" Well, here's where you get a chance to answer by dishing up the meat. In the paragraphs that make up this part of your proposal you'll:

- outline the material to be covered in your book

- explain your book's main points

- describe how wide or narrow your focus will be

- tell the editor exactly how the reader will benefit from having read the book.

Explain what you will include in your book. State the essential points you plan to make and describe the information you'll incorporate.

The author of *The Life and Times of the White-Bearded Gnu* might explain that he'll begin with two chapters that delve into the average gnu, including physical aspects, life span, indigenous habitat, natural enemies and diseases, and food sources, and then move into chapters about how he came to live with a herd of gnus, anecdotes from his daily life with the beasts, and what he learned from and about these animals during his time with them. He might then say he will wrap the book up with a chapter on the wildebeests' plight in trying to live in a world dominated by uncaring humans. This would, of course, be done in greater detail than the short summary I've given here.

Define the scope and breadth of your book. Will your book be a broad overview or will it focus on a single aspect of a subject? For instance, the gnu book might cover information collected on herds of white-bearded gnus from the 1950s to the present, or it might cover a time period of one month and the lives and actions of a single family of five animals. A book on plants might discuss general topics common to most plants, such as growth, seed development, photosynthesis, and osmosis, or it might focus on hybrid Dutch bulbs and how to get them to thrive in tropical climes.

Explain what the reader will get out of your book, that is, how having read it will benefit her. What problem will it solve or what need will it fulfill? What are the practical aspects? Will it be inspirational? Will she learn skills she can use to improve her personal relationships? Or will she learn of the best places to dine on a budget in Memphis, Tennessee?

The author of *The Life and Times of the White-Bearded Gnu* might point out that the reader will not only learn about white-bearded gnus, but about how humans can live synergistically in close proximity to animals of all kinds.

Nontextual elements

The New York Times used to be referred to as the "grey lady," because of its long unbroken columns of type. Modern publishers recognize that this type of design is hard to read and unappealing.

Besides adding substance to a book, photographs, illustrations, charts, sidebars, and quotes from well-known people that are set apart from the rest of the copy act as design elements, helping to alleviate this monotone effect. If your book will include any of these items—and I encourage you to—mention it here and estimate the number of each. For example:

Each chapter will have at least three photographs and there will be twelve sidebars spaced throughout the book.

Back matter

In this section of your proposal, include a sentence or two listing the back matter that will appear in the book. The term "back matter" encompasses anything that will be included after the main portion, or text, of the book. In the order that they usually appear, the standard items that constitute back matter include:

- appendix
- notes
- glossary
- bibliography (or suggested reading list)
- index

Not all books will, or should, have each of these parts, but including them tends to rachet up the value of your book to a reader. Librarians—who constitute a large market for books—especially like these to be included because of their usefulness to researchers.

You can simply mention that a notes section, bibliography, glossary, and/or index will be included. If you plan to include appendixes, list their titles and explain briefly what each will include. The back matter in this book starts on page 66.

This "meat" section of your proposal should run about two to six pages in length.

The potential market

Somewhere toward the top of your proposal—anywhere from in the lead itself to right after the "meat" section—tell the editor who makes up the pool of people likely to buy this book. The more people in this group, the better. This can be done in a straightforward manner, or it can be presented with a bit of flair.

For a book of accountant jokes:

> The Society of Certified Public Accountants has a paid membership of 347,000. Add to this the mass of men and women who do not hold a formal certification but are employed as accountants and the potential market for this book reaches into the millions. But consider also the friends and spouses of this crowd of number-crunchers and the total of potential buyers becomes astronomical.

For a book on selecting a spot for a family vacation:

> Hundreds of thousands of couples all over the nation face a recurring annual dilemma: Where should we go on vacation?

A great place to find numbers about how many people will be interested in your book is the *Encyclopedia of Associations*, available at most libraries. This directory lists information on an amazing number of associations related to nearly any subject, including how many people belong to the association. On the Internet, check out Weddles.com or type "associations on the net" in the Internet Public Library's search box at ipl.org.

Mention if your book has the potential of being adopted by instructors for use in courses they teach, or if it will have special appeal to librarians. Don't forget to explain why this potential exists, if it isn't obvious.

Don't Over Do It

Be guarded when predicting the appeal or the success of your book.

No book is a "book for everyone" or a "book for anyone wanting a good read." Books have distinct audiences. Yours will too, but it won't be a "must-read" for everyone.

During Oprah's reign as "Queen of Daytime TV," I must have read 111,239 nonfiction book proposals that predicted the author's book would become an Oprah selection, even though she mainly chose fiction. *New York Times* bestsellerdom is possible—we made it with *Dr. Gotts' No Flour, No Sugar Diet*—but rare.

Going overboard in estimating the appeal or success of your book will come off as the work of an unrealistic novice.

Style and voice

Spend a paragraph or two telling the editor what kind of style or voice you'll use in your writing. Will you write in a warm, fatherly way or in the voice of a crusty curmudgeon? Will the tone be conversational, like two good friends talking over a cup of coffee and cinnamon rolls, or will you use the voice of a Zen master instructing his student? Will you endeavor to break a complex, esoteric subject down using simple-language descriptions so a lay person can grasp its essentials? Or will your address be that of an academician?

Humor

And what about humor? This may simply be a personal preference, but I think nearly every book is improved by the inclusion of a bit of humor.

Rick Steves, who writes laudable travel guides, including *Rick Steves' Europe Through the Back Door*, plunks down bits of subtle humor in unanticipated spots throughout his books. For instance, in the section on French menu terms, he defines "lapin"(rabbit) as "bunny."He also takes credit for the large black-and-white kilometer markers that line the Rhine:"I put those up years ago to make this tour easier to follow...now the river-barge pilots have accepted these as navigational aids."

Other ways to add humor are to include humorous quotes, short jokes, or cartoons. Finding appropriate cartoons is easier today due to the searchable cartoon banks available on the Internet. While quotes and jokes often fall under the"fair use"doctrine or are in the public domain (see Copyright, page 24), most cartoons are copyrighted and you'll have to obtain permission to use them.

If you plan to insert a few chuckles into your book, mention it in your proposal.

Structure

In a paragraph or two, explain the structure you'll use in your book.

I find too many authors ignore this aspect of their book when writing their proposals. Perhaps they do this because they feel the structure will be obvious. Aren't biographies always chronological? Don't how-to books have a standard organization that begins with the simple and develops toward the complex?

The answer is, of course, no. The best books often have a structural twist that makes the book more interesting or more intelligible.

A biography might begin at a climactic point at the end of the subject's life and then flash back to the situations that occurred to cause this climax. A how-to book might start out with a glossary of terms with which the reader will need to be familiar, then be divided into three parts, each encompassing a single aspect of the book's subject, and a fourth part that brings it all together.

Perhaps for a book on the accomplishments of women in the twentieth century, you will write ten chapters, one for each decade, and you will open each chapter with a list of the names of the women you will cover in that chapter. Or, in an inspirational book aimed at teenagers, you'll include a photograph of a current teen idol and a quote from that person at the beginning of each chapter, and then proceed through two or three anecdotes illustrating how that person and a couple of others have dealt with a common situation in a teenager's life.

Author Jim Denney organized *Answers to Satisfy the Soul: Clear, Straight Answers to 20 of Life's Most Perplexing Questions* into four sections: "Questioning Ourselves," "Questioning Our Relationships,"'"Questioning Life,"and "Questioning the Infinite."Each section has five chapters. The twenty chapter titles are the twenty questions Denney addresses.

Besides helping the editor to visualize your book, detailing a well-thought-out and distinct structure suggests to an editor that you are an organized person who has given considerable thought to the book you're proposing to write.

> **"Don't make the mistake of saying yours is the only book on the subject or, worse yet, that you were unable to find any competing books."**

The competition

Identify your book's competition and explain why your book will be different or better.

Don't make the mistake of saying yours is the only book on the subject or, worse yet, that you were unable to find any competing books.

Yours will probably not be the *only* book on the subject, but let's just say, as an example, that you have written the only book on the white-bearded gnu. Even if no book has dealt exclusively with this (undoubtedly) fascinating creature, there will be books on other types of antelopes and books on African animals you can mention.

Saying you were unable to find any competing books just looks to an editor like you didn't bother to spend enough time searching, and he'll assume, if this is the way you work, it will be reflected in the book you write.

To find competing titles, check *Books in Print,* a multivolume listing of most books currently in print. *Books in Print* is available in larger libraries.

The search features of online bookstores such as Amazon.com are also useful when looking for competing titles. Of course, don't overlook brick-and-mortar stores, which, as a rule, stock only new titles and titles that have shown themselves to be consistent sellers. Knowing which titles are new and which are consistent sellers is helpful when you are faced with a plethora of titles and must winnow down the number you'll actually list in your proposal.

Use interlibrary loan to obtain a copy of titles that you don't wish to buy and that aren't on your local library shelves.

In your proposal, list full title and subtitle, author, publisher, year published, page count, size, binding (mass-market, trade paperback, hardcover), and price. Mention if the book is out of print (check Amazon.com). Then describe the book in two or three sentences and explain why yours will be different or better.

Be tactful and balanced in any criticism you include of another writer's book. Besides appearing as the mature and professional person you are, you avoid offending an editor who may like the book you're slamming or who may even have worked on the book himself.

In explaining why your book is better or different than the competition, you might point out that yours will be longer and more detailed than one, or shorter and written in an easier-to-read style than another. Yours may be written from the viewpoint of a parent, while an existing book is written from the viewpoint of a medical doctor. Yours may use actual case histories to illustrate the principles in it, while the other title just offers cold facts.

Be sure to point out when a similar title has sold tens of thousands of copies or has gone back to press numerous times. Look for sales figures in reviews, on the cover of the book itself—"*10 Million Copies Sold!*"—and in back copies of *Publishers Weekly*, especially its annual recap of winners and losers. This information may be on the author's website too.

To find out how many print runs a book has had, check the copyright page of the most current copy for something like "Fourth printing, 2011." Another common practice is for the print run to be designated on the copyright page by the last number in a series that looks like this:

10 9 8 7 6 5

In this case, the book would be in its fifth print run. If you are unsure if you have the most current copy, you can just write something like "...has gone back to press at least five times."

Here are a couple of fictitious examples of competing titles for our fictitious white-bearded gnu book:

Antelope Herding: An Epic Adventure in the African Wilderness, by Joanna Walsh. University of California Press, 1999, 325 pages, 6"x 9"trade paperback, $18.95. Out of print.

This expansive, well-written work tends to be a bit scholastic and fails to examine the interaction between man and animal. The illustrations and photographs are more limited than those that will appear in *The Life and Times of the White-Bearded Gnu*. This title enjoyed at least three printings before going out of print.

The Complete Book of Antelopes, by Daniel P. Jones. St. Martin's Press, 2009, 112 pages, 9"x 12"hardcover, $26.00.

This is more of a coffee-table type picture book than anything else. The book has beautiful photos, but the text lacks substance, providing only the most rudimentary information about the animals and their lifestyle and nothing about their interaction with man. A *Publishers Weekly* (January 14, 2012) article stated this book was the best-selling one in St. Martin's popular "Complete Book of Animals" series, with sales to date of 236,000 copies.

Your list of competing books should number between three and twenty. Be certain you include the most prominent books on your topic.

Prepublication endorsements/foreword

If you know someone who is an opinion maker or leader in the same field as your book's subject and who would be willing to write a foreword to your book or to supply a short endorsement—called a "blurb"—that could be used on the cover of your book or in the marketing of it, by all means mention it.

Forewords and prepublication blurbs by notable people not only influence prospective buyers—including librarians—they work to impress book reviewers that this is a book they ought to review. The fact that you can obtain a foreword or prepublication blurb from a significant opinion maker is another arrow in your proposal's quiver.

The key here is the person from whom you obtain the foreword or blurb needs to be an opinion maker who is somehow connected to the subject on which you're writing. If your second cousin is a United States senator and your book is on gardening, unless the good senator is a noted gardener, it'll just look strange to suggest in your proposal that you can get a senator to endorse your book.

For *The Longest Trek: My Tour of the Galaxy*, the autobiography of Grace Lee Whitney, who played Yeoman Janice Rand on the classic Star Trek series, Ms. Whitney obtained a prepublication endorsement from series star William Shatner. For a foreword, she tapped Leonard Nimoy.

Both of these men enjoy star recognition, but the person's name doesn't have to be a household word or even be recognized by a potential reader; often the person's title carries sufficient weight to influence the buying or reviewing decision. For *Hi! It's Me, Your Dog!*, author Lisa Mendoza obtained a blurb from Marion Lane, editor of the American Society for the Prevention of Cruelty to Animals' *Animal Watch*.

If you don't personally know someone you might ask, include a short wishlist of people you would like to have write a foreword or obtain an endorsement from, and mention you'll approach them as the project progresses.

Often the publisher can help you with contact information, or even make the request for you. For *California's Geographic Names,* compiled by David Durham, an expensive book aimed primarily at libraries in California, the Quill Driver Books' staff got a prepublication endorsement from Kevin Starr, the California State Librarian at the time. Naturally, Dr. Starr's title followed his name upon each use of the blurb.

> **"***The fact that you can obtain a foreword or prepublication blurb from a significant opinion maker is another arrow in your proposal's quiver.***"**

Promotion and publicity ideas

As I mentioned earlier, both large and small publishers expect authors to do a substantial portion of the promotion needed to sell the book. Many times it is the presentation of this section of the proposal that tips the scales for an author.

List the ways you can help to market your book. Be creative and comprehensive, but be reasonable. Don't, for instance, say you'll buy a half dozen full-page ads in *The New Yorker* unless you can convince the editor you have the finances to do so. Overpromising may make the editor think you're just a blowhard.

Include details on how you plan to execute your marketing strategy. For instance, if you travel around the country for your day job, name which cities you'll be visiting and explain how you plan to arrange talks, book signings, and appearances on local TV shows.

Here are just a few things you might promise you'll do:

- Put together a press kit and distribute it to targeted media.

- Set up and do radio interviews.

- Set up and do TV interviews.

- Produce seminars, with back-of-the-room sales.

- Contact associations interested in your book's topic, with an eye to getting a review in the associations' newsletters.

• Develop a social media marketing campaign. This likely would include:

  • Blogging

  • Interacting on others' blogs

  • Tweeting

  • Maintaining a Facebook and LinkedIn presence for yourself and the book

  • Maintaining a website

  • Writing a regular e-mail newsletter that would be sent to your list of subscribers and posted elsewhere.

• Hire a book publicist.

• Give talks on the local "rubber chicken" circuit.

• Contact businesses that might buy large quantities of your book to give to their employees or to use as a premium.

• Speak at industry or association conventions.

• Partner with a nonprofit group to conduct fundraisers at which the book will be sold.

• Locate an underwriter (a company, nonprofit organization, or individual interested in your book's subject) to purchase a quantity of books for free distribution to libraries.

• Write articles for publication that refer to the book.

• Set up and do book signings.

• Conduct a multicity tour.

• Write a newspaper column.

• Send copies of the book to opinion makers.

For more ideas to include in your proposal, consult *1001 Ways to Market Your Books* by book marketing guru John Kremer. I give a copy of this book to each of my authors.

Subsidiary rights

Subsidiary rights include rights sold or licensed to a third party. Usually, the author and publisher share in the net proceeds for these rights. Subrights sales are often the icing on the cake for both publisher and author, but sometimes it is only the sales of these rights that moves a book into the black for the publisher.

Subrights include but are not limited to:

- audio recordings

- television and feature film rights

- the right to publish the work in a foreign country

- the right to publish the work in a foreign language in this country

- serial rights, which is the right to excerpt part of a book in a periodical

- book club rights

- merchandising rights for products such as calendars or games.

We licensed foreign rights to the Quill Driver Books release *If You Want It Done Right, You Don't Have to Do It Yourself* by Donna M. Genett, Ph.D., to publishers in more than 15 nations on four continents. It's possible profits from these rights will surpass the profits from the book's sales in the United States.

If your book will have particular appeal to rights buyers, be sure to point it out in your proposal.

Is this a series?

Publishers love a series. Think of the *Chicken Soup for the Soul* books launched in June 1993 by Jack Canfield and Mark Victor Hansen. These two guys have stretched the series concept to new heights, with dozens of titles including *Chicken Soup for the Woman's Soul, Chicken Soup for the Teenager's Soul,* and *Chicken Soup for the*

Golfer's Soul. There's even one for you and me: *Chicken Soup for the Writer's Soul.*

Eighteen years later, mass retailer Walmart is still featuring end displays of the latest Chicken Soup titles in their book department.

To understate: The success of the *Chicken Soup* series has been quite pleasing to Canfield and Hansen's publisher, and other publishers would like to emulate this success.

If there is a follow-up book—sometimes called a "spin-off"—or a series of follow-up books which you would be willing to write, mention them here—giving potential titles and subtitles. If the decision makers at the publishing house really like the idea, you may end up with a multiple-book contract. And, even if they are only willing to consider one book at a time, suggesting a possible series—even a two-book series—is an enticement that is likely to work in your favor.

> **"***...suggesting a possible series—even a two-book series—is an enticement that is likely to work in your favor.***"**

Give a good deal of thought to the series idea, and spend nearly as much time deciding on titles and subtitles as you did on the book for which you're writing this proposal; suggesting a follow-up book that appears to be a weak sister may soften the appeal of the whole project.

And don't make the mistake of suggesting another book you'd like to write that is unrelated to this one. For that book, you should write a whole new proposal and market it to publishers separately.

Word count

Include a sentence that tells the editor the book's approximate length in words.

"Wait a minute," you protest. "Before I actually write my book, how will I know how long it's going to be?"

You won't; you'll just have to guess. After you've written a sample chapter to include in your proposal, use the word count

PERSISTENCE PAYS

"Anthologies don't sell."
"We don't think there is a market for this book."
"We just don't get it."
"The book is too positive."
"It's not topical enough."

With comments like these, Jack Canfield and Mark Victor Hansen's *Chicken Soup for the Soul* was rejected by publishers 140 times. In one particularly fruitless month, they set what may be a world record by having their book rejected thirty-three times, averaging more than one rejection a day—including Sundays. Finally their agent, who certainly deserves merit points for diligence, threw in the towel with "I can't sell this book—I'm giving it back to you guys."

Adjectives such as "determined," "tenacious," and "persistent" describe Canfield and Hansen. Most of us would have told ourselves we could take a hint and would have moved on to another book project or back to our day jobs, but not these two. Their next move was to attend the American Booksellers Association's annual trade show and convention (today known as BookExpo America).

At the show there were hundreds of publishers set up to showcase their wares. With more brass than bridle, Canfield and Hansen went from booth to booth hawking their book. (Note: This is *not* the preferred method for approaching publishers according to people who write books on how to write a book proposal.) One of the publishers they visited was Health Communications, Inc.

The rest is publishing history.

function on your word processor to determine the number of words in this chapter. Taking into account whether this chapter is a lot longer or a lot shorter than the other chapters you plan to include, multiply this word count times the total number of anticipated chapters. Round this number off to the nearest five thousand and put in your proposal a sentence worded something like:

> *The Life and Times of the White-Bearded Gnu: My Days Running with the Wildebeests* will run approximately 75,000 words.

The editor won't hold you to this exact length. He just needs to know approximately how long you plan for the book to be. Most nonfiction books run about 50,000 to 100,000 words.

Supplying an approximate word count is more exacting and appears more professional than supplying an approximation of the number of pages your manuscript will run.

Resources needed

Travel, polling, postage, research fees, copyright permissions, photography, illustrations, and long distance telephone calls are just some of the costs you may incur while researching and compiling your book. For the most part, costs of this nature are borne by the author.

Anticipate these costs, and if the anticipated amount is substantial, say $1,000 or more, include a paragraph explaining what the anticipated sum of all costs will amount to. If any of the individual costs are appreciable—say $500 or more—list these costs separately. Usually, the advance you receive from the publisher should include enough to cover these costs.

If you plan extensive use of copyrighted material, you may want to include the cost of obtaining the rights in your proposal. To figure out approximately how much copyright permissions will run, call the rights and permissions department of the publisher that published the material, or contact the author or authors directly. The rights and permissions person will often want to know the name of your publisher, what the first press run will be, and other details you won't know at this stage, so just ask her to give a ballpark figure. I find this first figure is often high and in the end can be negotiated downward.

If you plan to use only a small amount of copyrighted material, the charge will likely be too small to warrant researching it at the proposal stage. Often, you'll be allowed to use a small amount of material without any fee as long as you agree to correctly credit the source and perhaps provide a few free copies of the book. And don't forget, the use of some material, in some ways, doesn't require permission (see Copyright, page 24).

Estimated time to complete

Put in a sentence that reads something like, "A full manuscript including sidebars, will be completed nine months after receipt of a contract."

Anywhere from three months to twelve months will appear appropriate and probably be acceptable to an editor. Without extenuating circumstances—which should be explained—longer than twelve months may have a chilling effect, due to the fact most companies have annualized budgets and publishing schedules.

Saying something like "two weeks" will suggest you've already written the book—which is okay if you have, but then say so—or serve to make you look unrealistic.

There's a tendency to think the publisher will be in a hurry to receive the manuscript and thus for the author to overcommit. You know yourself best. If you're working a full-time job and only have nights and weekends to work on the book, figure accordingly. If the publisher would like the book sooner, he'll ask.

After you get a contract, be sure to keep your commitment, or let the editor know as soon as you discover you won't be able to do so.

Legal problems

Happily, most authors don't have to include anything in their proposal about potential legal problems, but, when the possibility does exist, it's best to bring it out into the open, and to have a plan for dealing with it.

Of the four most common areas of legal concern—copyright infringement, invasion of privacy, libel, and the dispensing of faulty advice—copyright infringement is the most easily dealt with. There are gray areas your publisher will help you navigate, but it's best, if you plan on using more than a modicum of any one piece of copyrighted material, that you plan on getting permissions.

Privacy and libel are stickier concerns. Anyone can sue for any reason, and even a successful defense of an invasion of privacy or libel suit can be quite costly to both publisher and author. Have your concerns checked out by an intellectual property rights attorney and state his name and his conclusions in the proposal, or list your concerns in the proposal and suggest you'll consult an attorney before entering into any agreement, if the publisher is interested in the book.

> **"Don't waste the editor's time with irrelevant information, like you enjoy skiing, or sing in your church choir, or live alone with your three cats, Muffy, Hildegard, and Genshiemer."**

When your advice has the potential to harm readers, explain in the proposal that you will present clear explanations and that you will tell the reader what precautions are necessary. The best defense against faulty advice is to not give it.

Anticipating that the editor is going to be concerned about these areas and explaining in the proposal how you will deal with his concerns may save the sale for you.

About the author

Repeat the information about yourself that you included in your query letter (see page 37). Expand on this information if appropriate. For instance, if you mentioned that you received a graduate degree from the University of Nebraska in political science, you might explain in the proposal that you wrote your thesis on a topic related to the one your book will be about.

Don't waste the editor's time with irrelevant information, like you enjoy skiing, or sing in your church choir, or live alone with your three cats, Muffy, Hildegard, and Genshiemer.

Table of contents

After your synopsis, put "Table of Contents" at the top of the next page of your proposal and list the parts, sections, and chapter titles (along with chapter subheads if you know them) in the order they will appear in your book. If your book will have a foreword written by another person, place his or her name after the listing for the foreword. List any back matter, such as appendixes, bibliography, notes, or index. When you are done, this page will look like the table of contents in most nonfiction books, but, of course, without page numbers.

Chapter-by-chapter outline

Next comes the chapter-by-chapter outline. In this section of your proposal, list each chapter title as it will appear in the book, and beneath each title, in a paragraph or two, outline exactly what that chapter will cover. List only the basic subjects the chapter will deal with. Try to keep your outlines succinct. A good rule of thumb is to write no more than one sentence for each page of text that you plan to have in the chapter.

Here's a sample chapter title and outline for the third chapter of *The Life and Times of the White-Bearded Gnu*:

Chapter 3. A Reluctant Hero

This chapter will explain how my reluctance to travel to Africa and take up a yearlong residency with the wildebeests was suppressed by my intense concern for the welfare of these magnificent animals and the gentle but persistent prodding from my wife.

The hardships of the journey will be recalled, including my bouts with seasickness, the constant vexation caused by a host of biting insects, the theft of my passport and money, and the humiliation of being arrested and held on vagrancy charges in a country that has a per-capita income that approximates what an average American spends on soda pop each year. Eventually, I meet and hire a native who, although unschooled and primitive in many ways, becomes my loyal companion and guide.

Sample chapters

Next in your proposal package come two to three sample chapters. The goal here is to show the editor you know how to write.

If this proposal were for a work of fiction, the sample chapters would have to be the actual first two or three in the book, but the nonfiction writer gets a break; you may include any chapters you wish. Since this is the case, if you have already written the whole book, select your best-written and most informative chapters.

If you haven't written the book yet, pick chapters to write that you feel will be the most interesting to read. These are usually the chapters you are most passionate about, and this passion usually comes out in your writing, making your proposal that much stronger. Don't fall into the trap of writing the chapters that you have the most information about, unless they are the also the chapters you can do the best job with.

If your book isn't made up of chapters per se (gazetteers, thesauri, encyclopedias, directories, etc.), include twenty to forty manuscript pages in lieu of sample chapters.

Supporting material

Some items you may choose to include:

- clips of your published work

- screen captures of your website or blog

- a list of your previously published work if it is extensive

- copies of reviews of your previously published books

• copies of photographs, charts, or other illustrations you'll include in your book

• copies of published material about yourself

• copies of newspaper or magazine articles about the topic, or about the size of the pool of prospective readers for your book

• brochures about seminars at which you were a presenter

• brochures about your business, if it applies to the book's subject

• your complete resumé, but only if it supplements the information you included in the "About the author" section of your proposal.

One agent I know says supporting material should always include a box of expensive chocolates, but I can't attest to the effectiveness of this practice in landing a contract.

Clips

Clips (clippings) aren't really clips; they're photocopies of clips. If you've written articles—particularly articles on the topic your book will address—including photocopies or, perhaps, screen captures (if the pieces appeared only online) at the back of your proposal may help to impress on the editor that you are indeed a professional-quality writer. And, of course, he gets to see yet another example of your fine prose.

If your writing experience is extensive, a list of the periodicals in which you've been published and the titles and publishers of the books you have written can well take the place of clips. If your previous books have received enthusiastic endorsements or reviews, include a photocopy of these items. If your books regularly appear on the *New York Times* best-seller list, skip the list and photocopies—as a matter of fact, skip the proposal, and just call me.

If you haven't written anything for publication, just ignore this part of the proposal. Avoid including a copy of the poem they printed in your high school yearbook or the letter to the editor your hometown newspaper published.

Proper manuscript format

Your book proposal should be formatted like a manuscript. This means 8½"x 11"white paper, one to one-and-a-half inch wide margins top, bottom, and both sides, with the text of the proposal double-spaced. Don't use a fancy or script typeface, and leave the right margin unjustified. As in your query letter, put your book's name in all-caps or italicize it.

Print only on one side of each sheet. Be sure to put the tag line, complete with page number, on all but the first page of your proposal. See page 106 for what your proposal should look like.

If submitting via an e-mail attachment, converting your document to an Adobe PDF solves potential problems with software versions, and PDFs are considered more virus proof, something most editors will appreciate.

Table of contents for the proposal itself

Most authors do not include a table of contents of the proposal itself, but I wish they would. I find a table of contents, especially when the proposal is lengthy, a useful tool that makes my job easier. And believe me, it's in your interest to make an editor's job easier.

Along the same vein, I encourage you to use subheads and bullets. A subhead is a brief explanatory headline that sets off sections of text."Table of contents for the proposal"is the subhead for this section of this book.

Bullets are the typographical elements that are used to set off lists and usually look something like this: •. (Most typefaces include a bullet character. In Windows-based programs, hold down the alt key and type 0149 to get a bullet; in Macintosh programs press the option key and type 8.) See the subsection"Supporting material," above, for an example of how bullets are used in this book. With a table of contents, subheads, and bullets, your proposal will be easier to read and appear more professional.

Don't staple the pages of your proposal or bind them in a 3-hole folder. The use of paper clips or similar fasteners is fine. If you wish, you can use a two-pocket folder to hold the loose sheets. This works well when you are enclosing clips or other elements with the proposal. How you arrange the material in the folder is up to you.

Sample Query Letter

Marc McCutcheon followed the standard "rules" for writing the following query letter *and* added a twist by splitting his hook between the lead and the postscript. Throughout this letter, he maintains a high ratio of ideas to words.

McCutcheon didn't include all the elements I suggest you include in a query letter, but he didn't have to; by the time I was through reading it, I was reaching for the phone.

As an exercise, why not try to identify the missing elements. Here's a list for your convenience:

- short letter
- strong lead
- high concept
- snappy title
- descriptive subtitle
- why this editor
- a synopsis
- who will buy this book
- how the author will help market it
- enthusiasm
- prepublication endorsements and/or foreword
- a short bio, including why the author is the one to write it
- the close

The answer appears after the query letter.

Stephen Blake Mettee
Quill Driver Books
1254 Commerce Way
Sanger, CA 93657

Dear Mr. Mettee:

The *high school dropout's* tour of the human body...
The *gay man's* guide to pleasuring *women*...
The *farmer's* cookbook...
The *housewife's* battle with obesity...
The *gym teacher's* belly flattener...
The *elderly woman's* adventure in solitude...
The *alcoholic's* chronicle of addiction...
The *home baker's* directions for giant cookies...
The elementary *schoolteacher's* encyclopedia of all things disgusting...
Best-sellers all...
Ordinary people all.
Working from kitchen tables and home offices across America.
The ordinary Jill or Joe from next door will be next. And if they're savvy, they'll figure out the secrets to doing this *full time.*

Damn, Why Didn't I Write That?: How Ordinary People Are Raking in $100,000 or More Writing Nonfiction Books & How You Can Too! tells how.

I *am* that high school dropout mentioned at the top of this page, and I've authored ten such nonfiction books and I *have* made $100,000 and far more. With no formal training of any kind. One international bestseller. Three Book-of-the-Month Club titles. Starred reviews in *Publishers Weekly.* Plus, reference books that will remain in print and collect royalties for not five or seven or ten years, but as long as *fifty years or more!*

There are *hundreds* more like me out there. Ordinary people (neither brainiacs nor workaholics) who have figured out a way to make a nice living from what I think is—hands down—the greatest home business anywhere on the planet: *Niche nonfiction book writing.*

Would you like to see the complete proposal and sample chapters? Please e-mail, write, or call, and I'll send you the whole package pronto.

One secret prevails above all, and I learned it early in my career: *Treat your writing as a business, not as a hobby, and you will be amply rewarded.*

I appreciate all your time and consideration. I look forward to hearing from you soon.

Sincerely,

Marc McCutcheon

P.S. People always worry that they don't have the proper "credentials" to write a book. When I tell them that one of the greatest-selling guides to sexually fulfilling women was written by two *gay* men, jaws drop with delicious incredulity.

If they continue to have doubts, I fall back on my "convincer": a how-to book that sold over six million copies in one year alone, and still stands as one of the fastest-selling nonfiction books of all time.

It was written by a *teenager*.

Did you find the missing elements?

Four elements are missing: why this editor; who will buy the book; how the author will help market it; and what prepublication endorsements and/or foreword might be gathered. Since McCutcheon was well aware that Quill Driver Books publishes books on writing and getting published, he was safe in assuming I would mentally fill in the blanks on the first two and the fourth missing elements.

As a publisher of writing books, I knew why he had chosen to send it to me, and, of course, I immediately understood who would be interested in buying such a book. He also could count on my understanding that his status as a best-selling author would help negate the need for a foreword by a noted person, and that both of us would know enough prominent people in the industry that we wouldn't have trouble acquiring prepublication endorsements.

As far as what he would do to help market it, I might have liked to see more there, but, since I was aware of his best-selling track record, I had little question that he'd perform gallantly in the marketing trenches.

Have trouble locating the high concept? It begins with "The ordinary Jill..." and continues through the next paragraph, which does double duty by introducing the title and the subtitle. By the way, *Damn, Why Didn't I Write That?* was selected for the Book-of-the-Month-Club as well as other book clubs and has remained in print for more than a decade.

Sample Book Proposal

Following is the book proposal that sold me on the idea of publishing *The Memory Manual: 10 Simple Things You Can Do to Improve Your Memory After 50* by Betty Fielding. (Note that the title changed along the way.)

Written a number of years ago, this proposal has withstood the test of time. As you can see, Fielding's lead is clear and concise. The first sentence does double duty as both her hook and her high concept. Editors like to hear that a book is doing something for the first time.

She also hit a hot button by saying the book would be a "popular trade book," that is, a book that will appeal to the general populace, because this is the type of book we like to publish. She then quickly outlined the book's main points and explained she would use anecdotes to liven up the text.

By the time I got to the fourth paragraph, I had a good feeling for what the book was about and was beginning to gain confidence in this writer's ability to bring both a high degree of organization and an economic use of words into her writing.

While Fielding's proposal isn't perfect in every aspect—I would have liked to hear a bit more on how she could help in marketing the book—as I read the rest of the proposal, I became convinced this title would work as the inaugural title in our trademarked "Best Half of Life" series for those over the age of fifty.

If you were to compare this proposal to the final book, you would find that as Fielding did the writing, the project metamorphosed somewhat. This is common. As long as the changes you incorporate as you research and write make the book stronger, the publisher is unlikely to complain. However, if you find you need to deviate from the proposal greatly, it would be wise to discuss this with your editor before proceeding.

(Fielding's actual proposal was double-spaced and included three sample chapters not included here.)

BOOK PROPOSAL

THE ART OF REMEMBERING AFTER FIFTY

BY
BETTY FIELDING

Contents   Page

Betty Fielding
Address
City, State Zip
Phone number
E-mail address

THE ART OF REMEMBERING AFTER FIFTY

PROPOSAL

OVERVIEW

THE ART OF REMEMBERING AFTER FIFTY brings together, for the first time in a popular trade book, the seven factors which research has shown work together to create and maintain a good memory. They are:

* understanding how memory works,
* discovering new tools for remembering,
* raising levels of motivation,
* solving problems of attention and concentration,
* organizing one's learning and lifestyle,
* taking care of physical, mental, and spiritual health,
* dealing with sensory and memory changes.

This book is unique also in building on the fact that levels of motivation play a critical role in memory. Anecdotes of real men and women (in fictitious contexts) make the program come alive. These people demonstrate that changes in attitudes, habits, and lifestyle patterns in the seven areas can increase memory power regardless of age.

Exercises are included for enabling the reader to examine personal priorities for setting goals which improve memory. As in any art, to achieve a goal involves commitment. It grows stronger with success, and this book is designed to help people succeed. In addition, making such changes can increase life satisfaction and may even save a life.

THE ART OF REMEMBERING AFTER FIFTY is a user-friendly program. It mobilizes natural resources for personal growth without resorting to artificial memory tricks such as encoding and nonlogical strategies. While these mnemonic devices continue to be the hallmark of traditional memory training after over two thousand years and are still being used in books on aging and memory, many people find them boring and unrelated to their daily lives.

I am well qualified to write this book because of my many years of teaching gerontology in colleges and universities and providing memory training in medical settings and senior centers.
THE ART OF REMEMBERING AFTER FIFTY is a program based on my review of research findings on aging and memory in the areas of neurology, psychology, biology, and the whole spectrum of health practices. I have field-tested the program, and numerous classes and lectures have generated many requests for a book which can be used for independent study.

Muriel James, Ed.D., coauthor of best-selling *Born To Win* (4 million copies sold) and twenty other books, has offered to write the preface.

This book will be completed in two months. Its length will be about 46,000 words, plus a bibliography and an index.

MARKET

There are three major audiences for this trade book:

* Mature adults desire to control their lives by having good memory skills and continuing to grow as long as they live.
* Families of older adults with memory problems will appreciate the up-to-date information about: ways of compensating for age-related memory changes; the effects of physical, mental, and spiritual health on memory; and the importance of regular contact with a doctor who can note symptoms requiring professional evaluation and treatment.
* Many members of the helping professions who have not received recent training in memory will appreciate this information in an easy-to-use format which they can apply in their own lives and recommend to their clients.

This book is also designed for use by classes in health care and retirement community settings. It will be a text for my classes, and a short manual could be written to assist other teachers in applying this unique program to the particular needs of their students.

Marketing possibilities include:

Modern Maturity, published by the American Association of Retired Persons, with a membership of thirty-three million. The six hundred thousand members of the National Retired Teachers Association receive a special edition of this publication.

Generations, Journal of the American Society on Aging, with over eight thousand members.

Academic Geriatric Resource Program Newsletter, University of California, Berkeley.

Turning Pages, the catalogue of the Center for Books on Aging, Serif Press.

My mailing list of former students and others requesting notification of publication.

COMPETITION

There are few trade books on aging and memory. Two of these have been recently reprinted with minor changes:

Don't Forget: Easy Exercises for a Better Memory at Any Age, by Danielle Lapp, provides for self-evaluation of memory skills and gives an overview of ways aging affects the memory process. The value of relaxation techniques to reduce anxiety is stressed. There are also chapters on absentmindedness, learning foreign languages, and remembering printed material.

Don't Forget focuses largely on mental exercises for improving awareness, attention, concentration, and organization of items to be recalled.

Improving Your Memory: How to Remember What You're Starting to Forget, by Janet Fogler and Lynn Stern, describes briefly how memory works, memory changes with aging, and factors affecting memory for all ages. There is a short section on Alzheimer's disease and other dementia. Most of this book is devoted to exercises for practicing memory tools.

(Nearly) Total Recall: A Guide to a Better Memory at Any Age, by Danielle Lapp, has a question-and-answer format addressing the most common concerns of adults about aging and memory lapses. This book supplies up-to-date information about the factors which affect memory and tools and tricks for maintaining and improving memory skills.

Memory Fitness Over 40, by Robin West, is an overview of the field of aging and memory from the background of a researcher.

It discusses how memory works and provides for self-evaluation. There is a section on Alzheimer's disease and other illnesses affecting memory. Strategies to compensate for age-related memory problems focus on improving attention, concentration, and organization. There are sections on remembering names, numbers, medications, and written material. This book is out of print.

Dealing with Memory Changes as You Grow Older, by Kathleen Gose and Gloria Levi, is a short book on memory strategies to compensate for age-related memory problems. It is also out of print.

None of these books deals in depth with all of the seven factors on which **THE ART OF REMEMBERING AFTER FIFTY** is based. In addition, none of them presents the latest research on the physical bases of memory and the effects of stress. Nor does any build on the fact that styles of motivation play a critical role in memory. Furthermore, none of them presents a comprehensive program of exercises for working toward goals related to the attitudes and lifestyle habits which create a good memory.

TABLE OF CONTENTS

Acknowledgments

Preface

Introduction

1. UNDERSTANDING HOW YOUR MEMORY WORKS

The Good News about Memory
Unravelling the Mystery of Memory
Your Memory at Work
Contents of Memory
Exercises: Identifying Goals for Your Memory Project

2. IMPROVING YOUR MEMORY WITH MORE TOOLS

Tuning in to Your Senses
Developing Mental Images

Using Words and Messages
Making Associations and Connections
Grouping
Practicing
Rehearsal and Review
Spacing Your Practice
Designing Memory Aids
Combining Memory Tools
Exercises: Memory Tools for Memory Power

3. SETTING GOALS AND MOBILIZING YOUR ENERGY TO REMEMBER

Motivation in Action
Your Natural Resources for a Memory Project
Sources of Motivation
Energy Problems
Fighting for Survival
Desiring Comfort
Searching for Meaning
Longing for Freedom
Yearning to be Free of Negative Feelings
Exercises: Using Your Resources and Energy For a Better Memory

4. SETTING MORE GOALS AND DISCOVERING MORE ENERGY TO REMEMBER

Enjoying Life for a Better Memory
Seeking Knowledge and Wisdom
Expressing Your Creativity
Developing Relationships
Desiring Something More
Interacting Urges
Exercises: Freeing More Energy for Your Memory Project

5. INCREASING YOUR POWER TO FOCUS AND CONCENTRATE

Attention and Concentration--Essential to Memory
Problems with Attention and Concentration
Distractions

Strategies for Better Attention and Concentration
Exercises: Focussing and Deepening Your Concentration

6. ORGANIZING YOUR LEARNING AND YOUR LIFE

The Power of Organization
Expanding Memory Through Lifestyle Change
Organizing Your Time
A Time Budget
Preparation for Future Recall
Organizing Your Surroundings
Exercises: Organizing to Improve Your Memory

7. TAKING CARE OF YOUR HEALTH

Good Health: Best News for Memory
Power of Good Diets
Physical Exercise and Memory
Exercise and Nerve Cell Growth
Mental Exercise Through Work and Play
Limiting Your Exposure to Toxins
Understanding Your Medication
Keeping in Touch with Your Doctor
Exercises: Health Practices to Improve Your Memory

8. DEALING WITH STRESS AND DEPRESSION

The Positive Value of Stress
Physical Impacts of Stress on Memory
Life Experiences and Stress
Strategies for Minimizing Distress
Reducing Depression to Improve Memory
Exercises: Feeling Good for a Better Memory

9. IMPROVING MEMORY IN SPITE OF AGING

Age-Related Sensory Changes
Memory Changes with Aging
Slowing of the Central Nervous System
Increased Distractibility
Shallow vs. In-Depth Thinking

Exercises: Identifying Sensory and Other Memory Problems and
Finding Solutions

10. BECOMING YOUR OWN MENTOR

Qualities and Gifts of a Mentor
The Art of Remembering--A Summary
Effective Contracts for Memory Projects
Exercise: Designing a Contract for Success in Improving Your
Memory

Bibliography

Index

CHAPTER SUMMARY

Chapter 1. UNDERSTANDING HOW YOUR MEMORY WORKS

People typically have more memory capacity than they
use. The first phase of a project to build a better memory is to
understand the memory process. This includes knowing how the
neural basis of memory affects a memory project and seeing how
the three stages of memory interact, together with the critical role
of working memory. These insights lead to increasing personal
awareness of memory at work. People can learn to improve both
incidental and intentional memory. Exercises to identify goals for
your memory project.

Chapter 2. IMPROVING YOUR MEMORY WITH MORE TOOLS

Memory tools are natural abilities and skills which people can
decide to use more often and more effectively. They are sensory
awareness, mental images, using words and messages, making
associations and connections, grouping, practice, rehearsal and
review, spacing, and using memory aids as reminders. Exercises to
develop memory tools for memory power.

Chapter 3. SETTING GOALS AND MOBILIZING YOUR
ENERGY TO REMEMBER

Seven basic urges generate the energies which motivate
people to work toward goals. Identifying and dealing with factors
which block or dilute these energies will improve the quality of
everyday life and increase memory power. Personal qualities which
contribute toward reaching goals include hope, courage, curiosity,
imagination, enthusiasm, caring, concern, and openness.

Two of these urges are the urge to live and the urge to be
free. The goals of the urge to live are to survive, to be comfortable,
and to find meaning in life. These goals can be directly involved in
improving your memory.

The urge to be free motivates people toward independence
and self-determination. This urge may involve physical and/or
psychological freedom. The hope for something more and the
courage to break free to learn in new ways are valuable allies in
the project of developing a better memory. Exercises using your
resources and energy for a better memory.

Chapter 4. SETTING MORE GOALS AND DISCOVERING
MORE ENERGY TO REMEMBER

Working toward other goals is also involved in improving
memory. The urge to enjoy aims toward happiness. The urge to
understand seeks knowledge. The urge to create moves people to
express themselves in their own unique ways. The urge to connect
finds fulfillment in friendship and love. These urges may work
together and are often directly related to memory functioning.

The urge to transcend involves the desire to be more, do more,
experience more than present reality. This urge underlies memory
improvement projects because of their roots in the need to grow
and solve problems. Exercises to free more energy for your memory
project.

Chapter 5. INCREASING YOUR POWER TO FOCUS AND
CONCENTRATE

Attention is selective, and concentration means sustaining
attention in order to collect the information needed or desired in
order to create a memory. Interference is a problem when two items
of information are confused, because they are very similar or occur

close together in time or space. Distractions may be internal or external factors blocking the memory process.

Making decisions and commitments to develop lifestyle habits which affect awareness, attention, and concentration will enhance the memory for people, places, and events. Exercises on focussing attention and deepening concentration.

Chapter 6. ORGANIZING YOUR LEARNING AND YOUR LIFE

"Don't agonize! Organize!" is good advice for anyone concerned about memory lapses. Five strategies for organizing your learning which increase memory power are

* developing a mind-set of curiosity and researching,
* breaking down a complex learning task into units,
* exploring a familiar interest in depth,
* using existing skills in a new setting,
* studying in a new field where you learn to think in unfamiliar ways.

Memory is also strengthened by organizing time. A time budget identifies ways of dealing well with priorities. Preparing to remember in the future involves

* making your calendar work for you,
* planning for special events and emergencies, and
* "priming the pump" to remind you of people's names and other items you want to recall.

Organization of your surroundings makes significant contributions to improving memory and preventing memory lapses. Exercises in organization to improve your memory.

Chapter 7. TAKING CARE OF YOUR HEALTH

Memory is supported by a healthy lifestyle. It consists of a nutritious diet, regular physical and mental exercise, limiting exposure to toxins, avoiding or limiting medications which affect memory, and keeping in touch with a doctor. Each of these factors makes a unique contribution to memory functioning. In particular, memory is very sensitive to any condition which interferes with the delivery of the oxygen and nutrients essential to brain cells. Exercises about health practices to improve your memory.

Chapter 8. DEALING WITH STRESS AND DEPRESSION

Stress is positive when it is a challenge acting as a stimulus to new learning and personal growth. Acute stress, which mobilizes the body against real or imagined threats, stimulates memory.

Chronic stress is often the result of personal losses—physical, psychological, social, or financial. Research has demonstrated that

* chronic stress damages important parts of the brain concerned with short-term memory; and

* people experiencing such stress can protect themselves through adopting positive attitudes, practicing stress reduction techniques, and making decisions around issues of control, predictability, social supports, and outlets for negative feelings.

Stress is often related to depression, which is the most frequent cause of memory problems. When this is treated, the person regains the capacity to enjoy life and memory skills function as before. Exercises on feeling good for a better memory.

Chapter 9. IMPROVING MEMORY IN SPITE OF AGING

Sensory changes and diseases that accompany growing older affect memory because of the critical role of the senses in acquiring information. Unless people find ways of coping with these problems, incomplete or inaccurate information will interfere with communication skills and memory functioning.

Three types of memory problems which accompany normal aging are

1. slowing of the central nervous system,
2. increasing distractibility, and
3. shallow processing of information, that is, the failure to think in-depth and look for meaning.

Decisions involving motivation, attention, concentration, and organizing learning, time, and surroundings can work together to more than compensate for these problems. Exercises on finding solutions to sensory and memory problems related to aging.

Chapter 10. BECOMING YOUR OWN MENTOR

An internal mentor gives support and sets realistic limits as you work on a memory project. The gifts of a mentor are permission, protection, and potency. Your mentor can reinforce a commitment to improving your memory.

Seven parts of a project to improve memory are

1. understanding how your memory works,
2. using a variety of memory tools and aids,
3. setting goals and working toward them,
4. focussing and concentrating on what's important,
5. organizing your memory and your life,
6. taking care of your health—body, mind, and spirit, and
7. becoming your own mentor.

Criteria for a contract to improve your memory are that it be reasonable, practical, and measurable. Exercise to design a contract for success in your memory project.

ABOUT THE AUTHOR

PROFESSIONAL ACTIVITIES AS EDUCATOR IN AGING AND MEMORY

Executive Director, Tri-City Project on Aging

University of California, Berkeley, Continuing Education Instructor Gerontology Certificate Program for Professionals:
"Psychology of Aging"
"Social Gerontology"
"Issues in Serving the Elderly"
Workshops:
"Adults with Aging Relatives"
"Senior Forum and Nutrition Site Staff Training"

John F. Kennedy University, Lecturer in Gerontology

Holy Names College, Lecturer:
"Staff Development in Working with Older People,"
"Women as Winners"

Western Gerontological Society, Community Education
Project:"Aging and Mental Health"

Diablo Valley College, Instructor and Lecturer:
"Preparation for Retirement"
"Fun after Fifty"
"Solving the Problems of Late Maturity"
"Nursing Home Ombudsman Training"
Contra Costa County (CA) Area Agency on Aging:
"Information and Referral Staff Training"

Contra Costa County Schools, training volunteers:
"Resocialization in Nursing Homes"
Wells Fargo Bank—San Francisco, Sacramento, and San Jose:
Workshops in "Preparation for Retirement"

Two medical centers, four senior centers lectures:
"Improving Your Memory—It's Easier Than You Think"
"Seven Steps to a Good Memory"

Recent Lectures on this memory program were presented at
the following:

California Council for Adult Education
California Association of School Transportation Officials
California Association of Retired School Business Officials
Alameda County medical groups, four sites
American Association of University Women, Danville
American Retired Teachers Association, Concord
Contact-Care Center, Lafayette
Chinese Community Senior Center, Berkeley
Rossmoor Retired Social Workers and Therapists

Recent TV Programs, Contra Costa Television:

"Memory Improvement for Older Adults," on *Senior Information Journal*, interviewed by Melissa McConnell, concerning memory issues with aging

Publications:

"Therapeutic Education with Older Adults." In *Techniques in Transactional Analysis for Psychotherapists and Counselors*, Muriel James and contributors. Reading, MA: Addison Wesley. 1979.
"Fun after Fifty with Ta." *Transactional Analysis Journal*, October, 1979.
"Aging: Transition and Challenge," *The Script*, February, 1982.
"Cultural Scripting and Aging," *Transactional Analysis Journal*. January, 1984.

Leadership:

University of California Extension, Berkeley
Curriculum Committee for the Gerontology Certificate Program for Professionals
American Society on Aging (Western Gerontological Society)
California Specialists on Aging
Contra Costa County Council on Aging
Mental Health Task Force
Housing Committee
Diablo Valley Foundation for the Aging
Lafayette Senior Services Commission

Education:

Smith College, B.A.
Lone Mountain College, M.A.
Other graduate work: University of California, Berkeley
University of Southern California, Andrus Gerontology Center
Continuing education in aging and mental health: American Society on Aging, CorTexT, and others.

"It's a brilliant piece of writing, Ted, but we feel that it might prove offensive to those who've been convicted of violent crimes."

Sample Agency Contract

The agreement between an author and an agent can take various forms. The one below is simply one example. In the contract below, the agent is appointed to represent all the works of the author. An alternative would be to limit the agent's representation to one book project only. (Used by generous permission of Jonathan Kirsch, author of *Kirsch's Handbook of Publishing Law*.)

Agency Agreement

Dated as of _____, 20__.

This Agency Agreement ("Agreement") is entered into by and between [Insert Name and Address of Agent or Agency] ("Agent") and [Insert Name(s) and Address(es) of Author(s)] (collectively "Author") and is based on the following terms and conditions.

Terms and Conditions

1. Author irrevocably appoints Agent as Author's sole and exclusive agent throughout the world to represent Author in any and all matters relating to the Author's Work, including but not limited to the negotiation of Contract(s) for the disposition of Author's Work. Author represents and warrants that Author is free to enter into this Agreement, and that Author has not entered into any other agreement or obligation which interferes with this Agreement.

2. "Author's Work," as the phrase is used in this Agreement, includes but is not limited to all ideas, story materials, characters, situations, formats, and works of authorship which Author has created or creates during the term of this Agreement, or in which Author has created or creates during the term of this Agreement, or in which Author has any title or interest, including but not limited to books, articles, playscripts, screenplays, teleplays, treatments and outlines, and any and all rights in and to such work.

3. "Contract(s)," as the word is used in the Agreement, includes but is not limited to any contract or agreement, whether oral or written, for the sale, license, option, or any other disposition or exploitation of

Author's Work, and/or any rights in and to Author's Work, in any and all media throughout the world.

4. Agent agrees to use her reasonable best efforts in representing Author under this Agreement. Author acknowledges and agrees that Agent has the right to represent other authors during the term of this Agreement.

5. This Agreement shall have an initial term of [Insert the Number of Months or Years of the Initial Term] from the date first written above, and shall be extended from year to year thereafter unless notice of termination in writing is given by one party to the other no less than sixty (60) days prior to the expiration of the initial term or any subsequent term. Such notice shall be given in writing by registered mail to the last known address of the other party. "Term," as the word is used in this Agreement, refers to the full term of this Agreement as it may be extended as described here.

6. Author hereby irrevocably authorizes Agent to collect and receive on Author's behalf all gross monies and other consideration due and payable to Author in connection with any and all Contracts. Agent shall pay such monies and other consideration, less commissions and expenses as provided in this Agreement, within ten (10) working days after receipt by agent.

7. Author hereby irrevocably assigns and agrees to pay to Agent, and authorizes Agent to deduct and retain as a commission for services rendered under this Agreement, a sum equal to [Insert Agent's Commission Rate] Percent of all gross monies and other consideration, whenever received, due and payable to Author in connection with any and all Contracts.

8. Author acknowledges and agrees that Agent may appoint subagents or others to assist her at her own expense. However, if Agent engages a coagent for the disposition of any particular rights in Author's Work, then a total commission of [Insert Joint Commission Rate] Percent shall be payable on any and all Contract(s) on which Agent and the coagent have jointly represented Author. Such commissions shall be shared between Agent and coagent according to their mutual agreement.

9. On any and all Contract(s) for the disposition of rights in Author's Work outside the United States and Canada, a commission of [Insert Commission Rate for Foreign Transactions] Percent shall be payable to Agent.

10. Author agrees that Agent is entitled to the foregoing commissions on any and all gross monies or other consideration paid or

payable to Author under (a) any and all Contract(s) which are entered into during the Term of this Agreement; and (b) any and all Contract(s) which are entered into within six (6) months after the termination of this Agreement, so long as the Author's Work which is the subject of such Contract(s) was submitted by Agent to the contracting party during the Term of this Agreement. Author further agrees that Agent is entitled to retain any and all commissions payable under this Agreement notwithstanding the fact that the publisher or other contracting party demands repayment of advances or royalties from Author.

11. If Author enters into one or more Contract(s) during the Term of this Agreement, then Author agrees that Agent will remain the sole and exclusive agent for all foreign and other subsidiary rights in the Author's Work which is the subject of such Contract(s) even if this Agreement is otherwise terminated.

12. In addition to commissions otherwise payable to agent, Author hereby agrees to pay Agent, and authorizes Agent to deduct and retain from all gross monies and other consideration payable to Author, the full amount of her out-of-pocket expenses incurred on behalf of Author, including but not limited to long distance telephone, postage, photocopying, telecopying, except that no expenses in excess of $250 shall be incurred without the Author's prior written approval. Upon termination or expiration of this Agreement, Author agrees to pay Agent any portions of such charges or expenses which have not yet been reimbursed.

13. Author hereby authorizes and instructs Agent to include a customary "agency clause" incorporating the terms of this Agreement in any Contract(s) which Agent may negotiate, and the parties agree to execute such additional documents as may be necessary to give full force and effect to this Agreement.

14. Agent and Author look forward to a long and mutually beneficial working relationship. However, in the event of any dispute under this Agreement, Agent and Author agree to submit their disputes to confidential binding arbitration under the rules of the American Arbitration Association in [Insert Location of Arbitration].

15. Agent and Author agree that this Agreement contains the entire agreement between them, and may not be modified or amended except by a writing signed by both parties.

Agreed and confirmed:
[Insert Names and Signatures of Author(s) and Agent.]

"Funny, funny, funny, but we're going to pass on 'How to Drink and Drive.'"

Sample Book Contract

This is only a sample contract. There are many variations. All contracts you as an author may sign need careful evaluation to be certain you understand and agree to the assignation of rights and responsibilities as spelled out in the contract. When in doubt, consult an attorney who specializes in publishing law.

For a detailed explanation of each clause in this contract, see *Kirsch's Handbook of Publishing Law*. (Used by kind permission of Jonathan Kirsch.) Annotations here are mine.

Model Publishing Agreement

Recitals

This Publishing Agreement ("the Agreement") is entered into as of [Insert Date Here] ("the Effective Date") by and between [Insert Name, Address and Legal Capacity of Publisher Here] ("Publisher") and [Insert Name, Address, Social Security Number, Date of Birth, and Citizenship of Author Here] ("Author") concerning a work presently titled [Insert Title Here] ("the Work") and described as [Insert Description of Subject Matter, Length, Etc.].

Grant of Rights

Author, on behalf of himself and his heirs, executors, administrators, successors and assigns, exclusively grants, assigns and otherwise transfers to Publisher and its licensees, successors and assigns, all right, title and interest in and to the Work, throughout the world, in perpetuity, and in any and all media and forms of expressions now known or hereafter devised, including but not limited to all copyrights therein (and any and all extensions and renewals thereof) for the full term of such copyrights, and all secondary and subsidiary rights therein.

Author, on behalf of himself and his heirs, executors, administrators, successors and assigns, exclusively grants, assigns and otherwise transfers to Publisher and its licensees, successors and assigns, all print publication rights in the Work in the English language, throughout the world, for the full term of copyright in and to the Work (and any and all renewals and extensions thereof). All rights not expressly granted to Publisher are hereby reserved by Author.

"Hardcover Rights," including the exclusive right to publish, or authorize others to publish, hardcover editions of the Work distributed primarily through trade channels such as bookstores and libraries.

"Softcover Trade Edition Rights," including the exclusive right to publish, or authorize others to publish, "trade paperback" or "quality paperback" editions of Work distributed primarily through trade channels such as bookstores and libraries.

"Mass Market Reprint Rights," including the exclusive right to publish, or authorize others to publish, softcover editions of the Work to be distributed primarily through independent magazine wholesalers and to direct accounts.

"General Publication Rights," including the exclusive right to publish, or to authorize others to publish, all of the Work, or excerpts, condensations, abridgments, or selections of the Work, in anthologies, compilations, digests, newspapers, magazines, syndicates, textbooks, and other works, and/or in Braille, either before or after first publication of the work in book form.

A shorter, more inclusive version of the above, which Quill Driver Books uses in order to address the ever-changing fields of e-book, electronic, digital, and other rights, reads:

The Author hereby grants, assigns and transfers to Publisher throughout the world the sole and exclusive right to print, publish, use, adapt, distribute, sell, lease, license, assign, dispose of or otherwise exploit the Work and all subsidiary rights in the Work, during the full term of copyright and any renewals, continuations and extensions thereof, in whole or in part, in all languages, and in any format or medium whether now known or hereafter devised.

Other publication rights that might be separately identified include: "E-book Rights," "Digital or Electronic Rights," "Foreign Rights," "Translation Rights," "Book Club rights," "School Editions," and "Large Print Editions."

"Subsidiary Rights"

This section may transfer to the publisher exclusive or nonexclusive rights involving what are often called "second or subsidiary rights." These rights include, but are not limited to: "Electronic Rights or Digital Rights,""Audio Rights,""Dramatic Rights,""Motion Picture Rights,""Television and Radio Rights," and "Merchandising Rights."

All of the rights granted by an author to a publisher can be limited by geographical territory, language, and term of the contract.

Copyright

Publisher shall, in all versions of the Work published by Publisher under this Agreement, place a notice of copyright in the name of the Author in a form and place that Publisher reasonably believes to comply with the requirements of the United States copyright law, and shall apply for registration of such copyright(s) in the name of Author in the United States Copyright Office.

Publisher shall have the right, but not the obligation, to apply for registration of copyright(s) in the Work published by Publisher elsewhere in the world.

Author shall execute and deliver to Publisher any and all documents which Publisher deems necessary or appropriate to evidence or effectuate the rights granted in this Agreement, including but not limited to the Instrument of Recordation attached hereto as an Exhibit to this Agreement.

Nothing contained in this Section shall be construed as limiting, modifying or otherwise affecting any of the rights granted to Publisher under this Agreement.

Manuscript

Author agrees to deliver to Publisher, not later than [Insert Delivery Date], two (2) double-spaced complete copies of the computer-generated manuscript of the Work in the English language ("Manuscript"), which Manuscript shall be of the length set forth in the Recitals and shall otherwise be acceptable to Publisher in form, content and substance.

On a date to be designated by Publisher, Author shall also deliver the Manuscript as otherwise described above on computer disk(s) in a size, format, and word-processing program language acceptable to Publisher. Author agrees to make and keep at least one (1) complete copy of the Manuscript and such disk(s).

Artwork, Permissions, Index, and Other Materials

Author shall deliver to Publisher, not later than the Initial Deliver Date unless otherwise designated by Publisher, each of the following materials:

Original art, illustrations and/or photographs (collectively "Artwork"), in a form suitable for reproduction. Subject to the mutual agreement of Author and Publisher, Publisher may acquire and/or prepare and include in the Work additional art, illustrations, photographs, charts, maps, drawings, or other materials, and the expense for such additional materials shall be allocated between Author and Publisher according to their mutual agreement.

Author shall deliver to Publisher, at Author's sole expense, written authorizations and permissions for the use of any copyrighted or other proprietary materials (including but not limited to art, illustrations and photographs) owned by any third party which appear in the Work and written releases or consents by any person or entity described, quoted or depicted in the Work (collectively "Permissions"). If Author does not deliver the Permissions, Publisher shall have the right, but not the obligation, to obtain such Permissions on its own initiative, and Author shall reimburse Publisher for all expenses incurred by Publisher in obtaining such Permissions.

Author shall prepare and submit, on a date to be designated by Publisher, an index, bibliography, table of contents, foreword, introduction, preface or similar matter ("Frontmatter" and "Backmatter") as Publisher may deem necessary for inclusion in the Work, and if Author shall fail or refuse to do so, then Publisher shall have the right, but not the obligation, to acquire or prepare such Frontmatter and/or Backmatter, or to engage a skilled person to do so, and Author shall reimburse Publisher for the costs of such acquisition or preparation.

Author acknowledges and confirms that Publisher shall have no liability of any kind for the loss or destruction of the Manuscript, Artwork, Frontmatter, Backmatter, or any other documents or materials provided by Author to Publisher, and agrees to make and maintain copies of all such documents and materials for use in the event of such loss or destruction.

Revisions and Corrections

If Publisher, in its sole discretion, deems the Manuscript, Artwork, Frontmatter and/or Backmatter, Permissions and/or any other materials delivered by Author to be unacceptable in form and substance, then Publisher shall so advise Author by written notice, and Author shall cure any defects and generally revise and correct the Manuscript, Artwork, Frontmatter and/or Backmatter, Permissions and/or other materials to the satisfaction of Publisher, and deliver fully revised and corrected Manuscript, Artwork, Frontmatter, and/or Backmatter, Permissions and/or other materials no later than thirty (30) days after receipt of Publisher's notice.

Termination for Non-Delivery

If Author fails to deliver the Manuscript, Artwork, Frontmatter and/or Backmatter, Permissions or other materials required under this Agreement, and/or any revisions and corrections thereof as requested by Publisher, on the dates designated by Publisher, or if Author fails to do so in a form and substance satisfactory to Publisher, then Publisher shall have the right to terminate this agreement by so informing Author by letter sent by traceable mail to the address of Author set forth above. Upon termination by Publisher, Author shall, without prejudice to any other right or remedy of Publisher, immediately repay Publisher any sums previously paid to Author, and upon such repayment, all rights granted to Publisher under this agreement shall revert to Author.

Editing and Publication Format

Publisher shall have the right to edit and revise the Work for any and all uses contemplated under this Agreement, provided that the meaning of the Work is not materially altered, and shall have the right to manufacture, distribute, advertise, promote, and publish the Work in a style and manner which Publisher deems appropriate, including typesetting, paper, printing, binding, cover and/or jacket design, imprint, title, and price. Notwithstanding any editorial changes or revisions by Publisher, Author's warranties and indemnities under this Agreement shall remain in full force and effect.

Proofs

Publisher shall furnish Author with a proof of the Work. Author agrees to read, correct, and return all proof sheets within seven (7) calendar days after receipt thereof. If any changes in the proof (other than corrections of Publisher's errors) are made at Author's request or with Author's consent, then the cost of such changes in excess of 5% of the cost of typesetting (exclusive of the cost of setting corrections) shall be paid by Author. If Author fails to return the corrected proof sheets within the time set forth above, Publisher may publish the work without Author's approval of proof sheets.

Time of Publication

Publisher agrees that the Work, if published, shall be published within eighteen (18) months of the Final Delivery Date, except as the date of publication maybe extended by forces beyond Publisher's control. The date of publication as designated by Publisher, but not later than the date of first delivery of bound volumes, shall be the "Publication Date" for all purposes under this Agreement.

Without limiting any other remedy of Author at law or equity, if Publisher fails to publish the Work within the time allowed, then all rights in and to the Work shall revert fully and wholly to Author, automatically and without notice, and Author shall be entitled to retain any and all advances and other amounts paid to date.

Author's Copies

Publisher shall provide Author with ten (10) copies, free of charge, of each edition of the Work published by Publisher. Author shall be permitted to purchase additional copies of the Work, for personal use only and not for resale, at the normal dealer discount, to be paid upon receipt of Publisher's invoice.

The author can often negotiate with the publisher to obtain a discount on books purchased by himself for resale. In fact, most publishers are happy when authors make "back-of-the-room sales" following speaking engagements, etc., and publishers are often very willing to allow the author to make the profit resulting from the discounted price.

Advance Against Royalties

Publisher shall pay to Author, as an advance against royalties and any other amounts owing by Publisher to Author under this Agreement, the sum of [Insert Amount Here] to be paid as follows: One-third upon signing of this Agreement, one-third upon delivery and acceptance of the complete Manuscript, and one-third upon publication of the Work in the first Publisher's edition.

Royalty on Publisher's Editions

Two models of royalty clauses follow. In the first, royalties are based on the retail cover price of a book, and in the second, royalties are based on the net revenues the publisher receives for sales of the book. Usually only one or the other model is used but mixing the two, say with print book sales earning royalties based on the cover price and e-book sales earning royalties based on net revenues, is not unheard of and may make more sense.

Royalties are where the rubber meets the road, and if you aren't using an agent and aren't completely familiar with trade discounts and the like, it might be wise to ask for advice and clarification from a intellectual property rights attorney.

Retail cover price-based royalties:

For each Edition of the Work published by the Publisher under this Agreement, Publisher shall credit Author's account with the following royalty on Net Copies Sold:

(i) _____% of the Invoice Price on the first 5,000 Net Copies Sold of any Edition,

(ii)_____% of the Invoice Price on the next 5,000 Net Copies Sold of any Edition, and

(iii)_____% of the Invoice Price on sales in excess of 10,000 Net Copies Sold of any Edition.

On bulk, premium, deep discount, and other sales at discounts of greater than _____%, and on direct-response sales, and other sales outside of the conventional channels of distribution in the book industry, Publisher shall pay one-half (½) of the royalty rate set forth above.

"Invoice Price," as the term is used in this Agreement, means the price shown on Publisher's invoices to its wholesaler and retailer customers from which the Publisher's wholesaler and retailer discounts are calculated. The difference between the Invoice Price and the suggested retail price or cover price as such price may be printed on the dust jacket or cover of the Work shall not exceed 5% without Author's consent.

"Net Copies Sold," as used in this Agreement, means the sale less returns of any and all copies sold by Publisher through conventional channels of distribution in the book trade, and does not include promotional and review copies, author's copies (whether free or purchased by Author), or copies for which a royalty rate is otherwise set forth in this Agreement.

"Edition," as used in this Agreement, refers to the Work as published in any particular content, length, and format. If the Work is materially revised or redesigned in any manner, or expanded in length or content, then the work as revised shall be considered a new "Edition" for purposes of this section.

Net revenues-based royalties:

For each Edition of the Work published by the Publisher under this Agreement, Publisher shall credit Author's account with the following royalty:

_____% of Net Revenues from the sale of any and all net copies sold.

"Net Revenues," as used in this Agreement, refers to money actually received by Publisher, for the sale of copies of the Work, net of returns, after deduction of shipping, customs, insurance, fees and commissions, currency exchange discounts, and costs of collection.

The inclusion of the deductions listed above is, perhaps, a bit weighted in favor of the publisher. Some likely can and should be negotiated away. Here, again, is where an agent can earn her keep.

Subsidiary and Secondary Rights

Except as otherwise provided below, Publisher shall credit Author's account with a royalty equal to 50% of all Net Revenues actually received by Publisher for the exploitation or disposition of Secondary and Subsidiary Rights in the Work.

Agency Clause

Author hereby irrevocably appoints [Insert Name and Address of Agent] ("Agent") as Author's sole and exclusive agent with respect to the Work which is the subject of this Agreement, and authorizes and directs Publisher to pay to agent all amounts owing to the Author under this Agreement, and to render to Agent all statements of account required under this Agreement. In consideration of services rendered by Agent, Author hereby authorizes Agent to receive, deduct, and retain 15% of gross monies paid to Author under this Agreement. Any sums payable to Author and paid to the Agent pursuant to this Section shall constitute a full and valid discharge of Publisher's obligation to Author with respect to such sums.

Author's Representations and Warranties

Author represents and warrants to Publisher that: (i) the Work is not in the public domain; (ii) Author is the sole proprietor of the Work and has full power and authority, free of any rights of any nature whatsoever by any other person, to enter into the Agreement and to grant the rights which are granted to Publisher in this Agreement; (iii) the Work has not heretofore been published, in whole or in part, in any form; (iv) the Work does not, and if published will not, infringe upon any copyright or any proprietary right at common law; (v) the Work contains no matter whatsoever that is obscene, libelous, violative of any third party's right of privacy or publicity, or otherwise in contravention of law or the right of any third party; (vi) all statements of fact in the Work are true and are based on diligent research; (vii) all advice and instruction in the Work is safe and sound, and is not negligent or defective in any manner; (viii) the Work, if biographical or "as told to" Author, is authentic and accurate; and (ix) Author will not hereafter enter into any agreement or understanding with any person or entity which might conflict with the rights granted to Publisher under this Agreement.

Author's Indemnity of Publisher

Author shall indemnify, defend and hold harmless Publisher, its subsidiaries and affiliates, and their respective shareholders, officers, directors, employees, partners, associates, affiliates, joint venturers, agents, and representatives, from any and all claims, debts, demands, suits, actions, proceedings, and/or prosecutions ("Claims") based on allegations which, if true, would constitute a breach of any of the foregoing warranties, and any and all liabilities, losses, damages, and expenses (including attorneys' fees and costs) in consequence thereof.

Each party to this Agreement shall give prompt notice in writing to the other party of any Claims.

No compromise or settlement of any Claims shall be made or entered into without the prior written approval of Publisher and Author.

In the event of any Claims, Publisher shall have the right to suspend payments otherwise due to Author under the terms of this Agreement as security for Author's obligations under this Section.

Author's representations, warranties and indemnities as set forth above and in this Section shall extend to any person or entity against whom any Claims are asserted by reason of the exploitation of the rights granted by Author in this Agreement, as if such representations, warranties and indemnities were originally made to such third parties. All such warranties, representations and indemnities shall survive the termination or expiration of this Agreement.

Advertising and Promotion

Publisher shall have the right to use, and to license others to use, Author's name, image, likeness, and biographical material for advertising, promotion, and other exploitation of the Work and the other rights granted under this Agreement.

Publisher shall have the right to determine the time, place, method, and manner of advertising, promotion, and other exploitation of the Work, except as Author and Publisher may set forth in a writing signed by both parties.

Author's Non-Competition

During the duration of this Agreement, Author has not prepared or published, and shall not prepare or publish or participate in the preparation or publication of any competing work that is substantially similar to the Work, or which is likely to injure the sales of the Work.

Option

Publisher shall have the right to acquire Author's next book-length work on the same terms and conditions set forth in the Agreement. Author shall submit a detailed outline and sample chapter of such to Publisher before submitting the work to any other publisher, and Publisher shall have a period of 30 days in which to review the submission and determine whether or not to exercise the option. The 30-day period described above shall not begin to run earlier than 60 days after the publication of the Work. If Publisher declines to exercise its option, then Author may submit the work to other publishers or otherwise dispose of the work.

Review by Publisher's Counsel

Notwithstanding any other provision of the Agreement, Publisher shall have the right, but not the obligation, to submit the Work for review by counsel of its choice to determine if the Work contains material which is or may be unlawful, violate the rights of third parties, or violate the promises, warranties and representations of Author set forth in this Agreement. If, in the sole opinion of Publisher or its counsel, there appears to be a risk of legal action or liability on account of any aspect of the Work, then Publisher may, at its sole option, (i) require the Author to make such additions, deletions, modifications, substantiation of facts, or other changes to avoid the risk of legal action or liability; or (ii) terminate this Agreement without further obligation, and Author shall be obligated to repay all amounts advanced by Publisher. Upon such repayment by Author, all rights granted to Publisher shall revert to Author. Nothing contained in this Agreement shall be deemed to impose on Publisher any obligation to review or verify the contents of the Work, or to affect in any way the warranties and representations of Author and/or the duty of indemnification of Author.

Copyright Infringement

If, at any time during the effective terms of this Agreement, a claim shall rise for infringement or unfair competition as to any of the rights which are the subject of this Agreement, the parties may proceed jointly or separately to prosecute an action based on such claims. If the parties proceed jointly, the expenses (including attorneys' fees) and recover, if any, shall be shared equally by the parties. If the parties do not proceed jointly, each party shall have the right to proceed separately, and if so, such party shall bear the costs of litigation. If the party proceeding separately does not hold the record title of the copyright at issue, the other party hereby consents that the action be brought in his, her or its name. Notwithstanding the foregoing, publisher has no obligation to initiate litigation on such claims, and shall not be liable for any failure to do so.

Accounting

Publisher shall render to Author a statement of account on the sales of the Work in all Publisher's editions, any other exploitation and disposition of rights to the Work, and other credits and debits relating to the Work and the rights granted in this Agreement, and pay Author any amount(s) then owing, as follows: (i) On or before September 30 for the previous six-month period from January 1 through June 30; and (ii) On or before March 31 for the previous six-month period from July 1 to December 31.

Publisher shall have the right to debit the account of Author for any overpayment of royalties, any and all costs, charges, or expenses which Author is required to pay or reimburse Publisher under this Agreement, and any amounts owing Publisher under any other agreement between Publisher and Author.

Publisher shall have the right to allow for a 20% reserve against returns. If royalties have been paid on copies that are thereafter returned, then Publisher shall have the right to deduct the amount of such royalties on such returned copies from any future payments under this or any other agreement.

As set forth in the Indemnity Clause above, in the event that any Claims are asserted against Author or Publisher, Publisher shall have the right to withhold royalties and other payments otherwise payable under this Agreement (or any other agreement between Author and Publisher) as a reserve pending a final determination thereof. Publisher shall have the right to apply any of such withheld royalties and other payments then or thereafter accruing to the reduction, satisfaction or settlement of such Claims.

Author shall have the right, upon reasonable notice and during usual business hours but not more than once each year, to engage a certified public accountant to examine the books and records of Publisher relating to the Work at the place where such records are regularly maintained. Any such examination shall be at the sole cost of the Author, and may not be made by any person acting on a contingent fee basis (other than the Author's literary agent during the course of the agent's regular and customary representation of Author). Statements rendered under this Agreement shall be final and binding upon Author unless Author sets forth the specific objections in writing and the basis for such objections within six (6) months after the date the statement was rendered.

Revisions

Author agrees to revise the Work as Publisher may deem appropriate during the effective term of this Agreement. The provisions of this Agreement shall apply to each revision of the Work by Author, which shall be considered a separate work, except that the manuscript of each such revision shall be delivered to Publisher within a reasonable time after Publisher's request for such revision.

Author may decline the Publisher's request to revise the Work, but if Author so declines, or if Author provides the manuscript of a revision of the Work which is unacceptable to Publisher, or should the Author be deceased or disabled, then Publisher shall have the right, but not the obligation, to make such revisions, or engage a skilled person to make such revisions, and Author (or, as appropriate, Author's estate) shall reimburse Publisher for all its actual costs of making such revisions. If Publisher engages one or more persons to make such revisions, then Publisher, in its sole discretion, may afford appropriate credit (including authorship or co-authorship credit) to such person(s).

Reversion of Rights

If the Work goes out of print in all Publisher's editions, Author shall have the right to request that Publisher reprint or cause a licensee to reprint the Work. Publisher shall have twelve (12) months after receipt of any such written request from Author to comply, unless prevented from doing so by circumstances beyond Publisher's control. If Publisher declines to reprint the Work as described above, or if Publisher agrees to reprint the Work but fails to do so within the time allowed, then Author may terminate this Agreement upon sixty (60) days' notice in writing. Upon such termination, all rights granted under this Agreement, except the rights to dispose of existing stock, shall revert to Author, subject to all rights which may have been granted by Publisher to third parties under this Agreement, and Publisher shall have no further obligations or liabilities to Author except that Author's earned royalties shall be paid when and as due. The Work shall not be deemed out of print within the meaning of this Section so long as the Work is available for sale either from stock in Publisher's, distributor's or licensee's warehouse, or in regular sales channels.

As I write this, with e-books and the capability of print-on-demand copies on the scene, the debate on how to establish that a title has gone out of print still rages. Here is how Quill Driver Books addresses the out-of-print question in a number of contracts:

The Work shall not be deemed "out of print" within the meaning of this Paragraph as long as it is available for sale either from stock in the Publisher's or licensee's warehouse or in regular sales channels, and/or by single copy sales through "print-on-demand" channels. If the work is only available as a "print on demand" and/or an e-book it will be deemed out of print if two successive accounting periods transpire without the Author being paid a minimum of $_____ in royalties.

The minimum amount is negotiable.

Remainders

If the Publisher shall determine that there is not sufficient demand for the Work to enable it to continue its publication and sale profitably, the Publisher may dispose of the copies remaining on hand as it deems best. In such event, Author shall have the right, within two (2) weeks of the giving of written notice by Publisher, to a single purchase of some or all of such copies at the best available price, and the purchase of film and plates at Publisher's actual cost of manufacture. If Author declines to purchase such copies, Publisher may dispose of such copies, and shall pay Author a sum equal to 5% of the amounts actually received by Publisher in excess of the costs of manufacture.

Rights Surviving Termination

Upon the expiration or termination of this Agreement, any rights reverting to Author shall be subject to all licenses and other grants of rights made by Publisher to third parties pursuant to this Agreement. Any and all rights of Publisher under such licenses and grants of right, and all representations, warranties and indemnities of Author, shall survive the expiration or termination of this Agreement.

Bankruptcy

If a petition in bankruptcy or a petition for reorganization is filed by or against Publisher, or if Publisher makes an assignment for the benefit of creditors, or if Publisher liquidates its business for any cause whatsoever, Author may terminate this agreement by written notice within sixty (60) days after any of the foregoing events, and all rights granted by Author to Publisher shall thereupon revert to Author.

Applicable Law

Regardless of the place of its physical execution, this Agreement shall be interpreted, construed and governed in all respects by the laws of the State of [Insert Name of State].

Modification and Waiver

This Agreement may not be modified or altered except by a written instrument signed by the party to be charged. No waiver of any term or condition of this Agreement, or of any breach of this Agreement or any portion thereof, shall be deemed a waiver of any other term, condition or breach of this Agreement or any portion thereof.

Notices

Any written notice or delivery under any of the provisions of this Agreement shall be deemed to have been properly made by delivery in person to Author, or by mailing via traceable mail to the address(es) set forth in the Recitals and General Provisions above, except as the address(es) may be changed by notice in writing. Author and Publisher agree to accept service of process by mailing in the same manner.

Right to Withdraw Offer

Publisher shall have the right to withdraw its offer of agreement at any time prior to delivery of this Agreement to and execution of this Agreement by Publisher.

Headings and Footers

Headings and footers are for convenience only and are not to be deemed part of this agreement.

Binding on Successors

This Agreement shall be binding on the heirs, executors, administrators, successors or assigns of Author, and the successors, assigns and licensees of Publisher, but no assignment by Author shall be made without prior written consent of Publisher.

Arbitration

If any dispute shall arise between Author and Publisher regarding this Agreement, such disputes shall be referred to binding private arbitration in the City of [Insert Location of Arbitration] in accordance with the Rules of the American Arbitration Association, and any arbitration award may be entered and shall be fully enforceable as a judgment in any court of competent jurisdiction. Notwithstanding the foregoing, the parties shall have the right to conduct discovery and the right to seek injunctive relief in any court of competent jurisdiction.

Attorneys' Fees

In any action on this Agreement, including litigation and arbitration, the losing party shall pay all attorneys' fees and costs incurred by the prevailing party.

Multiple Authors

Whenever the term "Author" refers to more than one person, such persons will be jointly and severally responsible for all duties, obligations, and covenants under this Agreement, and shall share equally in all royalties and other amounts to be paid under this Agreement, unless otherwise specified in a writing signed by all parties.

Entire Agreement

Publisher and Author acknowledge that they have communicated with each other by letter, telephone and/or in person in negotiating this Agreement. However, Author acknowledges and agrees that this Agreement supersedes and replaces all other communications between Author and Publisher, and represents the complete and entire agreement of Author and Publisher regarding the Work.

Advice of Counsel

Author acknowledges that Publisher has explained that he or she is entitled to seek the advice and counsel of an attorney or other counselor of Author's choice before agreeing to the terms set forth in this Agreement, and Publisher has encouraged Author to do so. Author acknowledges that, in the event Author signs this Agreement without seeking the advice of an attorney or other counselor, it is because Author has decided to forego such advice and counsel.

Riders and Exhibits

This Agreement consists of Section 1 through [Insert Number of Final Paragraph or Section] and the following Exhibits and Riders, if any: [Insert Description of Exhibits and Riders].

Signatures

IN WITNESS WHEREOF, Author and Publisher have executed this Agreement as of the day and year written above.

Nonfiction Book Proposal Checklist

Not all these elements appear in all book proposals, but the better proposals will include most or all. The items in bold are pretty much mandatory. (Make a photocopy of this page to use.)

- ❏ A table of contents of the proposal itself
- ❏ **A lead designed to hook the editor**
- ❏ **The high concept**
- ❏ **The title and subtitle**
- ❏ **An outline of the material, including the main points the book will cover**
- ❏ How wide or narrow the focus will be
- ❏ Names of experts who will supply prepublication endorsements or a foreword
- ❏ **The potential market**
- ❏ Style, voice, use of humor
- ❏ The book's structure
- ❏ **The competition**
- ❏ **Promotion and publicity ideas and how you'll help market the book**
- ❏ Possible subsidiary rights
- ❏ Possible spin-off titles
- ❏ **Anticipated word count**
- ❏ Resources needed (if any)
- ❏ Estimated time to complete
- ❏ Back matter to be included
- ❏ **An explanation of why you're the person to write this book**
- ❏ The proposed table of contents
- ❏ **Chapter-by-chapter outline**
- ❏ **Sample chapters**
- ❏ Supporting material

Standard Manuscript Format for a Book Proposal

There is no single, correct physical format for a book proposal, but following common format conventions, as shown here, is a good way to say to an editor: "I am a professional." Always use letterhead-sized, white paper. Always be sure the print is dark and legible. Paper clip sheets together or use a two-pocket folder; never staple. If submitting via an e-mail attachment, converting your document to a PDF is likely best.

Author's Name
Street Address
City, State Zip
Phone Number
E-mail address

Come down about one-third and type "Proposal for" and then the book's title and subtitle. Double-space and type "by" and the author's name.

PROPOSAL FOR *TITLE OF BOOK: SUBTITLE*

by Author's Name

Lorem ipsum dolor sit amet, consectetuer adipiscing elit, sed diam nonummy nibh euismod tincidunt ut laoreet dolore magna aliquam erat volutpat. Ut wisi enim ad minim veniam, quis nostrud exerci tation ullamcorper suscipit lobortis nisl ut aliquip ex ea commodo consequat.

Leave four blank lines, then start the text.

Duis autem vel eum iriure dolor in hendrerit in vulputate velit esse molestie consequat, vel illum dolore eu feugiat nulla facilisis at vero eros et accumsan et iusto odio dignissim qui blandit praesent luptatum zzril delenit augue duis dolore te feugait nulla facilisi.

Indent paragraphs.

Double-space text. Do not justify the right margin.

Lorem ipsum dolor sit amet, consectetuer adipiscing elit, sed diam nonummy nibh euismod tincidunt ut laoreet

Left, right, and bottom margins should be 1"-1½" wide.

Lastname/Title/4

Place a slug line: *last name/a key word from the title/page number*, one-quarter of an inch down, right justified, on all but first page.

dolore magna aliquam erat volutpat. Ut wisi enim ad minim veniam, quis nostrud exerci tation ullamcorper suscipit lobortis nisl ut aliquip ex ea commodo consequat. Duis autem vel eum iriure dolor in vulputate velit esse molestie

Leave 1½" blank at top of sheet, below slug line.

consequat, vel illum dolore eu feugiat nulla facilisis at.

END

Drop four lines below end of text on the last page and type "END."

The Author's Bundle of Rights

United States copyright law secures for the author owner-ship of a bundle of rights to his or her work. (Copyright laws differ from country to country, so be sure to review and understand your country's copyright laws. In most instances, many of the terms and concepts listed here will still be applicable.)

This bundle of rights may be divided and sold in any number of pieces and with any limitations the author can conceive of and get a publisher to agree to. The writer assigns or "licenses" the right to use the work to publishers, according to the contract between the writer and the publisher.

The following is just a brief summary of some of the compo-nents of the bundle of rights:

All rights—Just what it sounds like. When a writer licenses —or sells—all rights to a work to a publisher, the writer no longer has control in the future publication or licensing of the work.

Electronic or digital rights—These are terms used to define a bundle of rights related to computer technology. It may include the right to reproduce the material in e-book format, on various storage media, in web-based databases, in multimedia or interactive media, or with publishing-on-demand systems. Just like all other rights, an author may wish to assign certain electronic rights and retain others.

First serial rights—The right to be the first periodical to pub-lish the material in whole or in part. May be limited geographically.

Foreign language rights—The right to reproduce the material in one or more foreign languages. This also may involve geographic limitations.

Foreign rights—These include the right to publish the mate-rial outside of the originating country. These may be broken down by country or by some other geographical division, such as European rights, and may involve foreign language rights. With the advent of e-books and global retailers of e-books, foreign rights are still a bit dicey at the time of this writing, but standard conventions will be settled on.

Hardcover rights—Along with "trade paperback rights" and "mass-market rights," the right to publish the work in a certain print format. Sometimes limited geographically and in other ways.

Mass-market rights—See Hardcover rights.

North American rights—This limits the use of the work geographically to North America. May be used in combination with other limitations such as "North American, English language rights."

One-time rights—The right to publish all or part of the work, usually in a periodical, one time. Usually granted on a nonexclusive basis.

Second serial rights—Also called reprint rights. This gives a periodical the chance to publish all or part of a work that has already appeared in another periodical previously. Like one-time rights, these are usually nonexclusive.

Secondary rights—See Subsidiary rights.

Simultaneous rights—The right to publish the material at the same time purchased by two or more periodicals or publishers. This may be the case with magazines with noncompeting markets or, say, U.S. and Canadian book publishers.

Subsidiary rights—This is a term that refers any secondary rights including, but not limited to:

> Audio rights
> Book club rights
> Condensation rights
> Dramatic rights
> > TV rights
> > Film rights
> Mass-market paperback rights
> Merchandising rights
> Translation rights

Trade paperback rights—See Hardcover rights.

Selected Books

Every writer must have a good dictionary and thesaurus, but other books on the craft of writing and taking care of the business side of writing are almost as important. There are scores of good books available. Here are a few selected titles worth seeking:

The ABC's of Writing for Children: 112 Children's Authors and Illustrators Talk About the Art, the Business, the Craft, and the Life of Writing Children's Literature, by Elizabeth Koehler-Pentacoff.

1001 Ways to Market Your Books: For Authors and Publishers, by John Kremer. Much of the promotion for a book is left to the author. This is *the* book for savvy authors who want to make their books best sellers.

The Author's Guide to Building an Online Platform: Leveraging the Internet to Sell More Books, by Stephanie Chandler.

The Chicago Manual of Style. A big book that is often the final word on usage, punctuation, and form for authors, editors, copywriters, and proofreaders.

The Complete Guide to Book Marketing, by David Cole

Damn! Why Didn't I Write That? How Ordinary People are Raking in $100,000.00...or more Writing Nonfiction Books & How You Can Too!, by Marc McCutcheon.

Dan Poynter's Self-Publishing Manual: How to Write, Print and Sell Your Own Book, by Dan Poynter. This is the book most often recommended to aspiring self-publishers—with cause.

The Elements of Style, by William Strunk, Jr. and E.B. White. This thin volume provides concise instruction in the essence of good writing. If a writer can have only one book on the craft of writing in his or her library, this is the one. Read it and reread it.

Guerrilla Marketing for Writers: 100 No-Cost, Low-Cost Weapons for Selling Your Work, by Jay Conrad Levinson, Rick Frishman, and Michael Larsen. Provides highly effective, low-cost ways to promote your work.

Guide to Literary Agents, by Chuck Sambuchino.

How to Get Happily Published: A Complete and Candid Guide, by Judith Appelbaum. A classic.

How to Write & Sell Simple Information for Fun and Profit: Your Guide to Writing and Publishing Books, E-Books, Articles, Special Reports, Audio Programs, DVDs, and Other How-To Content, by Bob Bly.

The International Directory of Little Magazines & Small Presses, edited by Len Fulton. This annual lists over 6,000 paying and non-paying markets for your writing.

Kirsch's Handbook of Publishing Law: For Authors, Publishers, Editors and Agents, by Jonathan Kirsch. Covers the full spectrum of legal issues facing an author or publisher.

Literary Market Place (LMP) and *International Literary Market Place. LMP* is rather expensive. Most writers use their library's copy.

The Portable Writer's Conference: Your Guide to Getting and Staying Published, edited by Stephen Blake Mettee. Over 45 editors, agents, and authors provide insight on the craft and business of writing and getting published.

Secrets of Social Media Marketing: How to Use Online Conversations and Customer Communities to Turbo-Charge Your Business! by Paul Gillin

The Social Media Survival Guide, by Deltina Hay.

Write Your Book Now!, by Gene Perret. If you're having trouble completing your manuscript, get this book. It's a system that works.

Writer's Market, by Robert Lee Brewer. This book is a great place to check out the markets for your writing. Published annually.

Websites to Visit

Association of Authors Representatives—aaronline.org

The premier association for literary agents, AAR has a strict canon of ethics that all members must subscribe to. A searchable members list is available on the site. It's an excellent place to find an agent that is right for you. AAR has prepared a list of questions for an author to ask an agent *after* the agent has offered representation, but before signing with the agent (click on "FAQs").

Association of Authors Agents—agentsassoc.co.uk

For our U.K. readers, this is the United Kingdom counterpart to the United States' Association of Authors Representatives.

A Million Metaphors—AMillionMetaphors.com

The perfect metaphor, used in the perfect circumstance, is a spectacular thing. Add metaphors you yourself have given birth to or add your favorite metaphors written or said by others. Great resource to find just that right mental image. Brought to you by The Write Thought.

Book Marketing and Book Promotion—bookmarket.com

This is book-marketing guru John Kremer's seemingly endless site. Kremer wrote *1001 Ways to Market Your Book*, a tome without peer—get it and you'll see what I mean. If you haven't already, drop what you are doing and subscribe to his free e-newsletter.

Independent Book Publishers Association—IBPA-online.org

The leading association for independent book publishers. If you decide to self-publish, join this group before spending any money. The mistakes you *don't* make because of your membership will save you thousands.

Jonathan Kirsch—jonathankirsch.com

Intellectual property rights is a specialty, just as divorce work is. Don't confuse the two when seeking advice on publishing. Kirsch wrote the book on publishing law (actually two books): *Kirsch's Handbook of Publishing Law for Authors, Publishers, Editors and Agents* and *Kirsch's Guide to the Book Contract for Authors, Publishers, Editors and Agents.*

Quill Driver Books—QuillDriverBooks.com

Check out QDB's books and free reports on writing and getting published. Got a book you think might work for QDB? Download QDB's writer's guidelines.

Para Publishing—www.ParaPublishing.com

Self-publishing isn't for every author. Danger and frustration lurk at every turn. However, Dan Poynter's guide to self-publishing is a must-read for anyone thinking of going it alone. His site offers a wealth of free resources. Just for fun, see if you can figure out why he named his company "Para Publishing."

Society of Children's Book Writers and Illustrators—scbwi.org

If you write children's books, join this association for networking and mutual support.

The Write Thought—TheWriteThought.com
The Write Thought Blog—TheWriteThought.com/blog

Founded by the author of this book, The Write Thought is designed to support writers and publishers. Subscribe to The Write Thought blog for news and commentary on writing and publishing.

Shaw Guide to Writer's Conferences and Workshops—Writing. Shawguides.com

With more than 1,000 programs worldwide, if you can't find a conference that makes you drool here, you aren't serious about writing.

Writer Beware—sfwa.org/for-authors/writer-beware
Writer Beware blog—accrispin.blogspot.com

This group, sponsored by the Science Fiction and Fantasy Writers of America, "shines a bright light into the dark corners of the shadow-world of literary scams, schemes, and pitfalls."

Glossary

Advance—The amount a publisher pays an author before a book is published. The advance is deducted from the royalties earned. Often, an advance is paid in two or three parts: at the time the contract is signed, upon delivery of an acceptable manuscript, and, if in three parts, upon publication of the book.

Agent—An agent acts as the business representative/advisor for an author, handling such things as the submission of proposals to publishers, negotiating contracts, and tracking royalties. An agent generally retains 15 percent of what the author earns on a book project.

All rights—See The Author's Bundle of Rights, page 107.

Auction—Conducted—usually by an agent—when more than one publisher is interested in buying a book manuscript. Often conducted over a number of hours or days.

Back matter—The material at the end of a book, usually consisting of one or more of the following: appendixes, notes, glossary, bibliography, index. See also: Front matter.

Backlist—A publisher's list of books still in print. See also: Front list; Midlist.

Book packager—A company that puts together a book, working with writers, editors, graphic artists, and printers, but does not sell the book to the public, instead selling the package to a publisher.

Book proposal—Specific written information on a proposed book. Includes an outline, sample chapter or two, markets, and other such information.

Chapter book—Short, simple book used to graduate young readers from picture books.

Clips—Samples of an author's published work, usually photocopies of newspaper or magazine stories or articles.

Contributor's copies—Copies of a magazine or other periodical containing the author's work, often sent as partial or complete payment for the work.

Copyediting—Editing a manuscript for grammar, punctuation, sentence structure, etc., not content.

Copyright—Legal protection of an author's work. Under U.S. law, copyright is automatically secured when the piece is written. Copyright registration is not required for basic protection.

Conventional publisher—Contracts with an author for the right to publish his or her book, then edits, designs, prints, and markets the book at the publisher's expense. Pays the author royalties based on the book's sales. See also: Self-publishing; Subsidy publishing; Vanity publishing.

Co-publishing—See Subsidy publishing.

Cover letter—Short letter introducing a manuscript or proposal. Not always necessary. See also: Query/Query letter.

E-books—Any of a number of formats of books that are deliverable to e-readers, such as Amazon.com's Kindle, Barnes and Noble's Nook, or Apple's iPad. E-books may be straight text or enhanced with various features such as audio, video, search functions, and social media interactions.

Editor—Duties of editors differ from publishing house to publishing house. Often, editorial duties are shared by more than one person. Some editors acquire manuscripts for publication, others copyedit for things such as grammar and consistency. Content editors are concerned with the bigger picture, checking for omissions, conceptual problems, overwriting, and possible legal problems. Managing editors often are more involved in the business end of publishing. See also: Freelance editors.

El-Hi—Elementary school to high school market.

Fair use—Copyright law allows a small portion of copyrighted material to be quoted without infringing on the copyright owner's rights in some instances. See also: Plagiarism.

First serial rights—See The Author's Bundle of Rights, page 107.

Freelance editor—Freelance editors copyedit and content edit manuscripts on behalf of the author, commonly prior to the manuscript going to the agent or publisher. See also: Editors.

Frontlist—Books published in the current season. See also: Backlist; Midlist.

Front matter—Also called "preliminaries," this is the material at the front of a book, usually consisting of one or more of the following: title page, copyright page, dedication, epigraph, table of contents, list of illustrations, list of tables, foreword, preface, acknowledgments, and introduction. See also: Back matter.

Galleys—The first typeset proofs of a manuscript, used for proofreading and error correcting. A number of respected publications require galley copies of a book be sent to them three to four months prior to the publication date in order to be eligible for review in that publication.

Genre—General classification of writing, such as nonfiction, poetry, or novels, but primarily used to refer to categories within those: mysteries, science fiction, romances, business, children's, etc.

Ghostwriter—Author whose work is credited to someone else, by agreement. Autobiographies by famous people are often written this way, although it is now common for the ghostwriter to be acknowledged: By (famous person, in large print) with (ghostwriter, in smaller print).

Hard copy—Computer printout of material.

High concept—The high concept is the gist of your book distilled into one or two sentences. Often used in a lead in query letters and proposals, in verbal presentations to agents and editors and, when your book is published, it is often used in catalogs and brochures and by the publisher's sales representatives when presenting your book to retail and library buyers.

Hook—See: Lead.

ISBN—International Standard Book Number, the number printed on books used for ordering, sales, and catalogue information, usually used with a bar code that includes pricing.

Lead—The first few paragraphs of a query letter or proposal, designed to intrigue the agent or editor sufficiently that he or she reads the complete proposal. Sometimes called a "hook" because it is supposed to "hook" the reader.

Lead time—The time between the purchase of a manuscript and its publication.

Libel—A published accusation that exposes someone to contempt or ridicule, loss of income, or damage to reputation. Defenses include truth, consent, and fair comment. The publisher and the author can both be held liable.

List royalty—Royalty payment based on a book's list (also called retail or cover) price. Figured as a percentage. See also: Net royalty; Royalties.

Mass-market book—Books appealing to a wider market; these are the smaller-sized paperbacks sold in drugstores and supermarkets as well as bookstores. See also: Trade book.

Masthead—A listing of the names and titles of the staff of a publication.

Midlist—Nongenre fiction or nonfiction books that may make up the greater part of a publisher's list. Titles not expected to be blockbusters. See also: Backlist; Front list.

Model release—A form signed by the subject—or guardian of the subject—of a photograph granting permission to use the photo for the purpose stated on the form.

Ms, mss—Abbreviation for manuscript, manuscripts.

Multiple submissions—Sending a manuscript to more than one publisher or agent at a time. Same as simultaneous submission.

Net royalty—Royalty figured as a percentage of the amount a publisher receives for a book after various wholesale discounts have been granted. See also: List royalty.

On spec/On speculation—When an editor agrees to consider a book without committing to publishing it. Usually used by editors when they are unsure of a writer's ability or have not worked with the writer before.

Onetime rights—See The Author's Bundle of Rights, page 107.

Over-the-transom—Term for material sent by a writer unsolicited to a publisher; comes from the times when authors would toss manuscripts through an open window above a publisher's door in hopes of attracting an editor's attention.

Pen name—See Pseudonym.

Plagiarism—Copying another writer's work and claiming it as your own.

Proofreading—Careful reading of a manuscript to catch and correct errors and omissions.

Proposal—See Book proposal

Pseudonym—A name used on a work instead of the author's real name.

Public domain—Denotes material not protected by copyright laws. It may have never been copyrighted or the copyright may have expired.

Publishers—See Conventional publishing; Self-publishing; Subsidy publishing; and Vanity publishing.

Query/Query letter—A short letter to an editor or agent to propose a book.

Remainders—Copies of a book sold at a greatly reduced price when the publisher is overstocked or discontinuing the title or edition. Often the author receives no royalty, depending on the terms of the contract.

Reporting time—The time it takes an editor or agent to contact the writer regarding a query, proposal, or manuscript.

Royalties—Payment from a publisher to a book author based on the book's sales and the proceeds for such licensing rights as book club rights. For the publisher's sales of hardcover books, royalties generally range from 4–15 percent of the retail cover price; on paperbacks, it is 4–8 percent. See also: List royalty; Net royalty.

SASE—Self-addressed, stamped envelope, required with all manuscripts for return, or (if you don't want the manuscript back) the editor's reply.

Self-publishing—When the writer arranges for all the production and marketing for his or her book. It takes more money and energy up front and brings a degree of financial risk, but usually offers greater control, and the author/publisher gets to keep all the profits. Now seen as a legitimate alternative to traditional publishing. See also: Conventional publishing; Subsidy publishing; and Vanity publishing.

Sidebar—A short companion piece, separated from a book's text, that gives extra details or complementary information. Often typeset in a box. See page 35 for an example.

Simultaneous submission—See Multiple submission.

Slant—The emphasis or direction given to a work.

Slush pile—The large stack of unsolicited manuscripts often found in an agent's or editor's office. Usually, the slush pile is the last task in an editor's list of priorities.

Speculation—See: On spec/On speculation.

Subsidiary rights—See The Author's Bundle of Rights, page 107.

Subsidy publisher—A publisher who charges the author to typeset and print the book, but markets the book at the publisher's expense, usually along with the publisher's own titles. The publisher and the author share in any profits to the degree and by the method agreed upon in advance. This is often done with associations like historical societies. Comes dangerously close to vanity publishing and one should check out a subsidy publisher thoroughly before signing a contract. See also: Conventional publishing; Self-publishing; Vanity publishing.

Synopsis—A short summary of a novel or nonfiction book, perhaps one to two pages in length.

Tearsheet—The pages removed from a magazine or newspaper showing an author's work. So-called because the author tears the pages out of the publication to save for a clip file. See also: Clips.

Trade book—Hardcover or larger size paperback book. Generally denotes a book that is published to sell in bookstores and to libraries. See also: Mass-market book.

Trade paperback—The larger-size paperback book. Common trade paperback sizes are 8½" x 5½", 6" x 9" and 7" x 10".

Unsolicited manuscript—Any manuscript that an editor did not specifically ask to see. See also: Slush pile.

Vanity publisher—A vanity publisher charges an author to print and bind his or her book. Often this can be done for much less by going directly to a book manufacturer. (Book manufacturers are listed in *Literary Market Place,* available at your library.)

Vanity publishers often run adds in magazines and online that say something like "Publisher in need of Manuscripts." Vanity publishers rarely offer editing assistance and a vanity publisher's imprint on a book is the kiss of death with most potential reviewers. Often, a vanity press masquerades as a subsidy publisher, offering a very limited amount of promotion and marketing.

Versions of vanity presses have appeared online, often over-promising and pressuring an author to purchase add-on or upgraded services of questionable value. Vanity presses make their money off what the author will pay them, not from book sales. See also: Conventional publishing; Self-publishing; Subsidy publishing.

Word count—The number of words in a manuscript. Use a word processor's word count feature. Generally a double-spaced, typed document with one inch margins will have about 250 words per page.

Some standard word counts:

Nonfiction article	250 to 2,500 words
Nonfiction book	20,000 to 100,000 words
Novel	60,000 to 300,000 words
Novelette/Novella	10,000 to 50,000 words
Short story	1,000 to 10,000 words
Children's book	150 to 1,500 words
YA novel	15,000 to 50,000 words

Work for hire—Usually used to refer to the work of someone who is an employee of a company, but freelance writers can enter into this agreement in which the editor or other buyer purchases all rights to the writing. See also: The Author's Bundle of Rights, page 107.

Writer's guidelines—Formal statement of what a periodical or book publisher requires. Writers may send a note to the managing editor requesting the guidelines. Always include a SASE with such requests. Many writer's guidelines are available at the publisher's website.

YA—Abbreviation for young adult. Books, stories, or articles written for teenagers.

Index

About the Author

Stephen Blake Mettee, founder of Quill Driver Books and The Write Thought, is the editor of *The Portable Writers' Conference* and *The American Directory of Writer's Guidelines*, both Writers Digest Book Club selections, as is *The Fast-Track Course on How to Write a Nonfiction Book Proposal*.

Mettee has content edited (or rewritten, as the case may be) more than 150 books and has published scads of nonfiction articles, including a chapter in the 2004 *Writer's Market*. He holds a BA in Journalism.

During his fifteen years at the helm of Quill Driver Books, Mettee shepherded two titles into Book-of-the-Month Club selections and one onto the New York Times bestseller list. QDB's authors include names such as Irving Stone, Dr. Ruth Westheimer, Paul Gillin, Bob Bly, and America's most popular medical columnist Peter H. Gott, M.D., as well as many first-time authors.

Foreign rights to QDB titles have been sold in more than a dozen countries on four continents. QDB has been recognized by the industry periodical *Book Marketing Update* as one of the "Top 101 Independent Book Publishers" in the United States and by *Writer's Digest* as one the 100 most new-writer friendly book publishers in the U.S.

Every chance he gets, Mettee immodestly points out that this is quite a list of accomplishments for an independent house.

In 2008, Mettee sold Quill Driver Books to Linden Publishing in order to spend more time on other writing and publishing projects, but he still acts as acquisitions editor for QDB and, as such, is always in the market for exceptional nonfiction manuscripts.

Mettee is honored to serve as chairman of the board of The Independent Book Publisher's Association, the nation's largest book publishing association and the leading advocate for independent presses.

He regularly presents on writing and publishing in a number of venues nationally and internationally.

In 2011, The Write Thought launched AMillionMetaphors.com, a website on which authors, teachers, students, and others may find and share colorful and intriguing metaphors.

Please visit:
QuillDriverBooks.com
TheWriteThought.com & AMillionMetaphors.com

E-mail Steve Mettee at: Mettee@TheWriteThought.com

Great books on writing by
3-time Emmy winner GENE PERRET

Do you have a book burning inside you?
Can't get started writing? Can't finish?
Feel frustrated and need help?

Write Your Book Now!

A proven system to start and FINISH the book you've always wanted to write!

Gene Perret
Emmy Award-winning comedy writer and author of
The New Comedy Writing Step by Step

$15.95 ($17.95 Canada)

Write Your Book Now!

A proven system to start and FINISH the book you've always wanted to write!

—by Emmy Award winner Gene Perret

Whether you aspire to write a romance, an expert guide to business success, or the Great American Novel, *Write Your Book Now!* gives you proven, field-tested tools to successfully finish the book you've always wanted to write. *Write Your Book Now!* simplifies the book-writing project by breaking it down into a series of discrete tasks anyone can accomplish. Gene Perret, the author of over 40 books, helps you avoid distractions and delays, combat your emotional blocks, and establish and maintain a powerful writing momentum up to completion. Perret shows you the tricks and techniques professional writers use to produce finished manuscripts on time and stress-free.

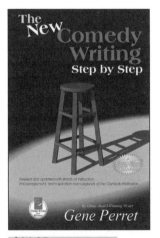

The New Comedy Writing Step by Step

Revised and updated with words of instruction,
encouragement and inspiration from Legends of the Comedy Profession

By Emmy Award-Winning Writer
Gene Perret

$14.95 ($19.95 Canada)

The New Comedy Writing Step by Step

A *Writer's Digest* Book Club Selection!

—by Emmy Award winner Gene Perret

Three-time Emmy Award winner Gene Perret's *Comedy Writing Step by Step* has been the manual for humor writers for 24 years. With this, his first update, Perret offers readers a treasure trove of guidelines and suggestions covering a broad range of comedy writing situations, along with many all-important insights into the selling of one's work. This new classic offers common sense, down-to-earth, practical tips to successful comedy writing.

66 Gene Perret is the world's top authority on comedy writing, thinking, and presentation. **99**
—Phyllis Diller

Available from bookstores, online bookstores, and
QuillDriverBooks.com, or by calling toll-free 1-800-345-4447.

Must-have writers' references from Quill Driver Books

$14.95 ($16.95 Canada)

Books, Crooks and Counselors

How to Write Accurately About Criminal Law and Courtroom Procedure

—by Leslie Budewitz, mystery writer and attorney at law

Books, Crooks and Counselors is an easy-to-use, practical, and reliable guidebook that shows writers how to use the law to create fiction that is accurate, true-to-life, and crackling with real-world tension and conflict. Leslie Budewitz, a practicing lawyer (and mystery writer) with over 25 years of courtroom experience, will teach you the facts of legal procedure, what lawyers and judges really think about the law, and authentic courtroom dialogue.

❝ Clear, concise, and infinitely useful … The ultimate mystery writers handbook! ❞

—Laura Childs, *New York Times* bestselling author of *Fiber & Brimstone* and *Scones & Bones*

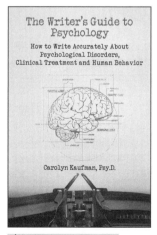

$14.95 ($16.95 Canada)

The Writer's Guide to Psychology

How to Write Accurately About Psychological Disorders, Clinical Treatment and Human Behavior

—by Carolyn Kaufman, Psy.D.

Written by a clinical psychologist who is also a professional writer and writing coach, *The Writer's Guide to Psychology* is an authoritative and easy-to-use reference to psychological disorders, diagnosis, treatments, and what really makes psychopathic villains tick.

The only reference book on psychology designed specifically for writers, *The Writer's Guide to Psychology* presents specific writing dos and don'ts to avoid the misunderstandings frequently seen in popular writing.

❝ This book should be in every writer's professional library and every clinician's, too — whether writers or not! ❞

—*New York Journal of Books*

Available from bookstores, online bookstores, and QuillDriverBooks.com, or by calling toll-free 1-800-345-4447.

Professional books for working writers from Quill Driver Books

$15.95 ($17.95 *Canada*)

How to Write & Sell Simple Information for Fun and Profit

Your Guide to Writing and Publishing Books, E-Books, Articles, Special Reports, Audio Programs, DVDs and Other How-To Content

—by Robert W. Bly, author of over 70 classic marketing books

How-to writing is the easiest and most lucrative field an aspiring writer can enter—and copywriting legend Bob Bly is sharing his secrets to how anyone can become a successful how-to writer. *How to Write & Sell Simple Information for Fun and Profit* is a step-by-step guide to building a profitable new career.

❝ Grab this book and devour it. It just might be the catalyst that changes your life. ❞

—Herschell Gordon Lewis, author of *Internet Marketing: Tips, Tricks and Tactics*

$24.95 ($27.95 *Canada*)

The Social Media Survival Guide

Strategies, Tactics, and Tools for Succeeding in the Social Web

—by Deltina Hay

This is a book for do-it-yourselfers—authors, publishers, and everyone else who wants to promote themselves through social media marketing. *The Social Media Survival Guide* focuses on proven tools that create specific results. Here are specific strategies, tactics, and tools that will help you reach a global audience and communicate with readers and reviewers personally and effectively. You'll get step-by-step, specific advice on WordPress sites, podcasting, social networking and more.

❝ The most authoritative, comprehensive, and technically accurate guide I have ever seen to social networking.❞

—Bob Bly, author of over 70 classic marketing books.

Available from bookstores, online bookstores, and QuillDriverBooks.com, or by calling toll-free 1-800-345-4447.